Tales from the Trails

Tales from the Trails

Mostly true stories of changed lives (and socks) in the wilderness of the West, featuring those who survived the author's adventures

T. Duren Jones

Foreword by Kevin J. Anderson

WordFire Press
Colorado Springs, Colorado

TALES FROM THE TRAILS
Copyright © 2014 by T. Duren Jones

All rights reserved. No part of this book may be reproduced or transmitted in any form or by any electronic or mechanical means, including photocopying, recording or by any information storage and retrieval system, without the express written permission of the copyright holder, except where permitted by law. This novel is a work of fiction. Names, characters, places and incidents are either the product of the author's imagination, or, if real, used fictitiously.

ISBN: 978-1-61475-184-7

Cover design by T. Duren Jones
and
Art Director Kevin J. Anderson

Book Design by RuneWright, LLC
www.RuneWright.com

Published by
WordFire Press, an imprint of
WordFire, Inc.
PO Box 1840
Monument CO 80132

Kevin J. Anderson & Rebecca Moesta, Publishers

WordFire Press Trade Paperback Edition 2014
Printed in the USA
www.wordfirepress.com

Contents

Dedication i
Acknowledgments iii
Foreword v
Introduction ix
Steep Cliffs and Frozen Feet 1
    Castle Valley Overlook, Moab, Utah
If You Slip, You Will Die.. 5
    Vernal Fall, Yosemite National Park, California
Life and Death in 12 Falls Canyon 11
    Bailey Canyon, San Gabriel Mountains, California
One (Breathless) Step at a Time! 17
    Quandary Peak, Tenmile Range, Colorado
Spires, Surprises and Smelly Boys 21
    Ansel Adams Wilderness, Sierra Nevada, California
Lost Canyons and Large Toilet Bowls 33
    Needles District, Canyonlands National Park, Utah
Grin and Bear It 37
    Culebra Peak, Sangre de Cristo Range, Colorado
The Start with a Finish.. 41
    Colorado Trail, Beginning and End, Denver to Durango
The Playful Hand of God, and Joe 45
    Joshua Tree National Park, Mojave Desert, California
Mistakes Happen 49
    Crestone Peak, Crestone Needle, Humboldt Peak, Sangre de Cristo Mountains, CO
The Upside Down Mountain 59
    South Rim, Grand Canyon, South Kaibab Trail to Bright Angel Trail
Camping with Cannibals 67
    Colorado Trail, Segment 14, Chalk Creek Trailhead to US-50

Tales from the Trails

I Fall Down a Lot 75
    Longs Peak, Front Range, Colorado
Carpe Diem, but Before Nightfall 79
    Chesler Park Loop, Needles District, Canyonlands, Utah
Chili Rellenos & Heroes Who Soared 83
    Kit Carson Peak/Challenger Point, Sangre de Cristos, CO
Mischief in Moab 87
    Canyonlands and Arches National Parks, Utah
Blown Away 95
    Cameron Point, Mosquito Range, Colorado
The Marine and the Giant 99
    Castle Peak, Elk Mountain Range, Colorado
Marching On! 111
    Colorado Trail Segment 8, Tennessee Pass to Camp Hale
Revenge of the Old Man on the Mountain 115
    Huron Peak, Handies Peak, Colorado
Two Tickets to Paradise 125
    Windom Peak, Sunlight Peak, South Mount Eolus, Chicago Basin, San Juan Mountains, CO
Best Laid Plans 131
    Canyonlands, Island in the Sky, Moab, Utah
Fatty McButterbutt vs. the Thunderstorm 145
    Sawtooth Ridge, Mount Evans to Mount Bierstadt, and Back Again
Twisted Logic 153
    Mount Herman, Pike National Forest, CO
Making Lists and Punishing Friends 159
    El Diente Peak, San Miguel Mountains, Colorado
Conquering Contrast Canyon 167
    Lathrop Canyon, Island in The Sky, Canyonlands, Utah
Conclusion 177
One More Step… 179
About the Author 181
Other WordFire Titles 183

Dedication

This book is dedicated, with love, to my dear wife, Diane. She has believed in me for just about every endeavor I've set my mind on—no matter how harebrained at times. Diane sacrificed time and resources for me to climb all the Colorado 14ers, worried about me on every trip, and has not only supported me in my writing passion, but also kicked my rear end to keep me going. I want to thank Diane for her backing, organizational skills and good content suggestions. Her involvement in this process was indispensable, and she has always been my best fan for anything in life.

Diane is my best friend and has been my trail companion countless times, even though that wasn't her favorite activity. We had an agreement, however: She would hike with me; I'd go shopping with her. I got the better end of the deal.

Acknowledgments

My sincere apologies—and gratitude—to friends and family who participated in my trail adventures but fortunately lived to tell about it. I may have put you through some unpleasant ordeals in my quests. Thank you for memories to last a lifetime, and for not beating me senseless with a hiking stick along the way.

I could not have written these stories without the help and support of many. My best buddy since the third grade, Bruce Peppin, believed in me enough to set writing deadlines and make little flags of encouragement to display on my desk for motivation.

Special thanks to my writing group guys, Ray Seldomridge and Gino Martinelli, who thought I could do something ridiculous like putting out a book. They regularly gave of their time, resources, funny margin commentaries (to keep my feet on the trail), keen observations, and great edits. Without their good word doctoring, I'd have fallen off a literary cliff.

My appreciation goes to Kevin J. Anderson and Rebecca Moesta for this publishing opportunity. And thanks to Kevin (who is featured in several stories) for his inspiration and passion for the outdoors that spurred me on to explore more paths less traveled. Thanks to Lou Moesta for providing excellence in proofreading, making me look better than I am.

I must also express gratitude heavenward. One simply cannot spend time out in nature, in the wilderness, surrounded by beauty and splendor, without sensing something greater, and pausing to say "Thank you."

Foreword

Getting away from it all—and getting to the heart of it all.

So far the dentist appointment has been the best part of the day—and that should tell you what kind of day it was. Numerous deadlines, complications, and administrative details as the publisher of Wordfire Press; several new releases coming out at once as well as some major revisions to a six hundred page novel manuscript of my own; a looming deadline for an entirely different (an entirely unfinished) novel manuscript and travel arrangements for a convention appearance; ninety-six story submissions to read for two anthologies my wife and I are editing ... and on top of it all getting a new crown put on at the dentist. Bombarded by all that, as I was driving back home from the dentist appointment, I saw how beautiful it was outside. A Colorado February day: sixty degrees, blue skies, only a few patches of un-melted snow remaining, it made me recall how long it had been since I went hiking

Which of course reminded me that I had to write this introduction for my hiking partner and brother-in-law Tim's book. Sigh. Another deadline. Then I realized that writing the introduction was not actually a burden—but an opportunity. Rather than being locked in my office, strapped to the keyboard to fight back the constant flood of emails or to wince each time the phone rang with someone requesting "just a quick little thing," I could think about all of the wonderful hiking adventures I'd had done with Tim. And since I do all of my writing by dictating into a digital recorder, I could actually go outside in this beautiful day, walk along a few wonderful trails, breathe the fresh air, listen to the trickle of melting snow. No, that wasn't a burden at all. I could get away from it all, I could be outside, surrounded by beautiful Colorado scenery and just recharge my batteries.

When my wife and I had moved to Colorado seventeen years ago, I was already an avid hiker in California, but I did most of those hikes alone, climbing Half Dome in Yosemite, Mt. Whitney, Lassen Peak, wandering dozen miles of trails in King's Canyon or Sequoia National Park, exploring the deserts of Death Valley. Tim and his family had moved to Colorado a few years ahead of us. An avid hiker and outdoorsman, he had done plenty of exploring on his own and had discovered many places that I simply had to see.

On the Christmas before we moved to Colorado, Tim gave me two books, a set of books as a gift. Trails and instructions on how to climb all fifty-four of the mountain peaks in Colorado that were over fourteen thousand feet high, comma dubbed the "Fourteeners." Tim had decided to climb them himself and was hoping for a hiking partner. I spent that winter (as many forlorn hikers do) looking at the guidebooks, reading descriptions of trails and imagining myself out there on those dotted lines, wending their way up ridges, over saddles, and up to the final ascent.

When we did move to Colorado that following July, I already had my marching orders and Tim had his plans. Although I did climb some of those peaks solo, Tim and I ascended many of them together. We tried to get friends to join us, most of whom had insufficient lung capacity or endurance. We did the harder and harder ones. Each summit had its own unique character; each name checked off on the list felt like another triumph. While staying in shape throughout the winter season we would go snowshoeing up around Rocky Mountain National Park or in other high mountain trails. We'd exchange tips and maps of new places we had discovered, new trails to explore.

As a prolific writer, I produce several novels a year and numerous short stories and articles. To me when I'm out on the trail, I find the inspiration to describe alien worlds and interesting characters. In the silence and the solitude, I can walk for miles and dictate dozens of pages.

After we finished all the Fourteeners, Tim and I decided to tackle the Colorado Trail. Nearly five hundred miles winding through the most beautiful mountainous terrain in the state. As of this writing, we've done all but one segment, only twenty miles left, and you can bet we'll finish it this summer.

Tim and I have a system down, how we'll walk together, but far enough apart so that I can have the concentration I need to dictate my stories and he can revel in the beautiful scenery and take all the photos he likes. Oftentimes we'll start at opposite ends of the trail and hike toward each other and swap cars on the way home.

We both find the wilderness a place to get away from the chaos and pressure of modern life, from deadlines and bills and family obligations. It's an environment where we can simply get to our roots, clear our heads and just be filled with all the majesty around us.

Even though we're both in our fifties, we can do things that most of our peers can't. A few years ago, we drove to Arizona and hiked down to the bottom of the Grand Canyon and back up in a day, passing signs warning us not to do that and winded, muscular German hikers who were struggling to keep up. Twenty more miles in a day is no longer an impossible challenge, we would simply do it and we work hard to stay in shape so we can keep doing these things we enjoy so much.

And even though there are times we are snowed in, trapped by a raging blizzard close to the summit of fourteen thousand foot Columbia Peak, huddled between rocks and shivering; or dancing across the treacherous Sawtooth Ridge that connects Mt. Evans and Mt. Bierstadt as thunder rumbles and lightning flashes all around and the hair stands up on our heads and arms; or when we're plodding along through a Noah-worthy downpour with miles to go before we reach our cars, it's all part of the adventure. While dangling on ropes climbing a six hundred foot sheer dry waterfall on the face of Little Bear Peak, or when Tim missed the trail turn off and walked for miles out of the way (after already having hiked sixteen miles that day), we still wouldn't trade that for anything.

When I tell these stories to my wife, Rebecca, she doesn't understand why we would consider that to be "fun." But if you have to ask, you won't understand. There's something indefinably special about walking hard for hours and hours, reaching a saddle and seeing a pristine and untouched vista of mountain and valleys spreading out in front of you, knowing that you are quite likely the only human being within miles. It's not just to get away from all the frenzy of modern life, it's to get in touch with your core.

It's good for your soul.

Tim has discovered that and this book includes some of his most heartwarming and nerve-wracking adventures. Some of them include me without (much) exaggeration. Some of them are escapades and insights Tim had with other companions or just by himself.

I hope you enjoy the vicarious journey and I hope that Tim and I continue to have real outdoor adventures of our own.

— Kevin J. Anderson —

Introduction

"Thousands of tired, nerve-shaken, over-civilized people are beginning to find out going to the mountains is going home; that wilderness is a necessity."

— John Muir —

Colorado was a perfect fit for my wife, Diane, and me, and our four young, adventurous children, Sarah, Cary, Daniel and Spencer. My family and I moved to colorful Colorado in 1991 with my job, and we never looked back. One bumper sticker echoed our sentiments: "I wasn't born in Colorado, but I got here as soon as I could." The kids could fall out of trees, slip on skates, or fly off cliffs just as easily here as in California, but with fewer crowds and a lovely background.

We immediately embraced the regional and statewide outdoor activities offered in such a beautiful part of the United States. As often as we could, we camped, biked, fished, went bouldering, rafted, hunted, and hiked. A lot of hiking. In these 20-plus years we have logged hundreds of miles on trails, and I'm still discovering and enjoying new ones.

To love the outdoors as we do was just an extension of our former Southern California lifestyle. We took all the kids out to the wilderness—starting in backpacks—at a very early age. And they all survived my wacky escapades.

Even though Greater Los Angeles is nothing but city in every direction for hours, we lived at the base of the San Gabriel Mountains, east of Pasadena, which gave us an easy way to "get away from it all," even if just for an afternoon. On other occasions we would pack the kids up in an old Plymouth station wagon (piled up so high with camping stuff that it looked like something out of the film *The Grapes of Wrath*) and our "Green

Machine" would sputter, cough and steam, but eventually get us to family camps, state parks, and national wonders like Yosemite National Park.

As a kid, I was always outdoors, especially during the summertime. My friends and I wanted to—had to—*find* things to do. These were the days before so much digital electronics occupied kids' time. We rode our bikes for miles, built forts, swam at the public pool, played "Kick the Can" with neighborhood kids late into the evening (until our parents shouted from the porch that it was time to come in), and hiked our mountain foothill trails. I knew my life would somehow always be about exploring the wild places.

My brother-in-law, Kevin J. Anderson, and my sister-in-law, Rebecca Moesta, the writers, also moved to Colorado. Having hiked just about every trail in California from Death Valley to Yosemite, Kevin apparently decided he needed new scenery and challenges. Plus, Rebecca's parents had moved to Colorado too.

I suggested to Kevin that we tackle all 54 of Colorado's 14,000 ft. peaks. When we finished those, he recommended that we hike the 468 miles of the Colorado Trail—The CT. He also introduced me to trail trekking in Moab, Utah—now one of my favorite places to "get lost." Kevin's passion for the outdoors matched mine, and through the years, I think we've both pushed each other to go higher and farther. Many of our adventures together are captured in the pages that follow.

I am not inherently a risk taker. I don't deliberately go looking for life-threatening experiences. (Okay, I guess it could be argued that the half dozen or so Class Four difficulty level 14er climbs fit that category.) I don't bungee jump, paraglide, scuba dive, or shop department stores the morning of Black Friday.

In some cases, the challenges, or even dangerous aspects, of wilderness journeys just come with the territory. That's what makes it wild, after all. Slip happens. Storms surprise. Bones break. Rocks fall. Trails disappear unexpectedly. And what doesn't kill you makes for great storytelling!

This book was written to share my love for the outdoors, and to recount some of the many adventures I've been able to have with friends and family on wilderness trails all over the American West. I've also touched on some valuable lessons for life that I learned on the trail.

I hope the book will inspire you to get outdoors yourself, rather than scare you off. I made the effort to experience the riches of the wilderness (and survived to tell the tales). You can too. Meanwhile, may you take pleasure reading these mostly-true accounts as much as I enjoyed living them.

Steep Cliffs and Frozen Feet

Castle Valley Overlook, Moab, Utah

"No enemy is worse than bad advice."

— Sophocles —

"The trail is well marked. Improved recently. Just a few mile loop, that's all. Fun and easy."

Sure. 150 years ago, our lodge host could have sold snake oil to gullible pioneers arriving in the Southwest. Is it really good for repeat business to send guests off to their wilderness doom? Who rebooks a room then?

My brother-in-law, Kevin, and I started across the road from our accommodations with enthusiasm. The previous winter day, we had legged about 15 miles in the Needles District south of Moab in Utah, so this desert canyon trail jaunt sounded simple and enjoyable.

Kevin is a best-selling fiction author, *New York Times* list status. He often creates *other* worlds based on some of his treks on this globe. The Moab region is one of those places for his inspiration. It's like walking on another planet. When Kevin and I hike together, I give him enough distance for his recording/writing (he hikes and speaks into a digital recorder to write his chapters). Presumably, I'm asked to stay back a ways so I won't listen in and then return home and tweet plot point spoilers from his next novel.

This time we decided we'd traverse the terrain on this undemanding loop in opposite directions and meet in the middle. Perfect plan. I would take the high ridge portion first; Kevin the bottom of the canyon stream route.

This all sounded good until I discovered halfway up my 800 ft. elevation climb that I could not go around a steep snowfield, but had toe-dig steps to carefully pass through it. Oh, and about that easy, well-marked trail? Forget it. This was Sir Edmund Hillary mountaineering stuff! One slip and I'd have a terminal-velocity slide down to a rocky demise. (Okay, I exaggerate, but it was scary.)

It took unexpectedly long to reach the knobby summit. I had thought Kevin would have met me by now from his counter-clockwise route. I was rewarded with extraordinary views of Castle Valley and the snow-capped La Sal Mountains in the distance. With dusk approaching, I couldn't stay to enjoy the panoramic vistas. And where in the (canyon) world was Kevin? This plan wasn't working out well. Had he turned back? Had he sprained an ankle? Considering his hiking experience, I knew he couldn't be lost. Still, I was concerned.

Castle Valley Overlook Point, Utah
High point of an otherwise frustrating hike.

I pressed forward. I couldn't go back through that snowfield, especially in the dark. And I had to find Kevin, hopefully not facedown somewhere along the icy streambed. If I could find the trail, I could see footprints in the canyon snow, or lack thereof, and determine his progress and route.

Every attempt to get down to the creek was met with a cliff edge. I had to improvise, moving up and down canyon ledges, looking for a way out. And now, I was searching in the dark by flashlight. I'm pretty good at route finding, but this was ridiculous.

Well meaning, or terribly delusional, individuals had placed cairns—stacked stone trail markers—everywhere and anywhere along the steep drop-offs, but nowhere did the paths descend to the creek bed below. Using my small flashlight and connecting the rock pile dots, I found that trails twisted back up the side of the mountain, doubled back on themselves, and if mapped out, I was sure it would have looked pretzel patterned. Whoever designed this route should have been ticketed with a TMUI (trail marking while under the influence). Perhaps it was some deranged or disgruntled former lodge employee.

I was relieved to finally get down to the creek, but encountered thick brush and ice-covered rocks. I pushed through the leafless branches—grabbing at me like some skeletal wraiths—and tromped fresh snow along the creek edge. Downstream I discovered two sets of boot prints, one coming, one going, which, if followed, would take me back to the road and on to the lodge.

I was surprised at what a serpentine path I was following as I tracked the footprints. I stayed higher on the bank, but it was clear my predecessor had crossed back and forth over the creek many times, traversing the slick, ice-covered stepping stones. At one point, it appeared that the other hiker had tried to scramble up a muddy slope in a frustrated attempt to escape the cold stream, only to return to the original wet route as the barely acceptable, but most expedient way out.

I did make it back to my lodge room and was pleased to find the lights on and somebody home. There I found Kevin, thawing out, blow-drying his soaking boots, his jeans still frozen stiff on the floor. He had changed into dry clothes, turned the room heat to the volcanic setting, and had a writer's few choice words for our host's advice for an "easy" hike.

The boot prints I had seen in the snow alongside the icy creek were Kevin's. If I thought my part of the trail was poorly marked, his was worse. His path would end abruptly at the base of a cliff, take him into impassible thick brush, or have him crisscross the stream several times on slick rocks or logs. He had slipped off the rock steps and splashed into the frigid water so many times, he finally gave up and just crossed *through* the creek several times on his way back to the lodge. We agreed that his decision to turn back was a good one, and would guarantee future Kevin J. Anderson novels.

We both had great adventures, to be sure, and a few laughs. But we would research and double check recommendations for unfamiliar hikes in the future.

If You Slip, You Will Die
Vernal Fall, Yosemite National Park, California

*"Providence protects children and idiots.
I know because I have tested it."*

— Mark Twain —

Our oldest son, Cary, probably shouldn't be walking this earth today. He was always our risk-taker, the super-curious one, the adventurer and explorer, and the one we should have left at home with Grandma (for his own safety) when we went hiking or camping.

Cary always had to climb the highest boulder, build the largest campfire (in turn creating the biggest marshmallow torch known to man), and flip over every rock in search of some gross, wiggly, biting thing-y to examine. He'd be the overeager kid at the front of the group at a ranger talk with his hand raised and waving for attention even before it was time for questions.

In truth, we enjoyed and encouraged his youthful quest for knowledge and understanding of our incredible world. His mother, Diane, and I loved his energy and curiosity, and cheered on his exploration of nature's wonders. I was a good parent, in this regard. And also an idiot.

Why I thought it was a good idea to take three young children, aged 3, 5 and 7, up the mile and a half trip to the top of Vernal Fall in Yosemite National Park still perplexes me to this day. Getting there all sounded so idyllic at the time: The *High Sierra* Loop; *Happy Isles* Bridge; the *Mist* Trail; and on to the *Emerald* Pool. Who wouldn't want to go there? This was the wilderness equivalent of Pinocchio being tempted to go to Pleasure Island! I could be forgiven for my lack of good judgment, right?

The day started out fine. No sign of the black bear that had been chased out of the campground the night before by a flash-mob of temporary residents creating a cacophony of sounds with clanging pots, blown whistles, beaten logs, and hurled insults about ursus bad hygiene, eating habits, drooling, snorting, small tails and such. I felt kind of sorry for the poor guy. Just a bear doing bear things. No reason for the cruel, personal attacks.

We were tent camping in the crowded valley with friends and woke early to a crisp, cerulean, cloudless sky. We even had an accident-free hot breakfast and camp cleanup time. Very little bickering, punching or throwing things. And the *kids* behaved themselves, too. No fresh boo-boo's to cover with Hello Kitty bandages. An unusually good beginning to our day of anticipated adventure.

It did amaze us that Cary could be covered head-to-sandals in campfire soot within five minutes of bouncing Tigger-like out of the tent. Day One we cleaned him up frequently. But after a time, what was the point, really? We just let him stay like that for the rest of the week. He seemed happy enough, looking like a mini coal miner after a 12-hour shift.

We rode the free shuttle—shoulder-to-shoulder with kids on our laps—to the Happy Isles Nature Center. Ah, a happy place, just like Disneyland, only more jam-packed. Hikers in Hawaiian shirts, short-shorts (and that was the men—this was the 80s, after all) and flip-flops poured out of numerous tour busses, mesmerized by the beauty, like lemmings running *up* a cliff to their death.

People actually do die on Vernal Fall and Nevada Fall (its cousin farther up) each year. Having not done my homework on this seemingly important bit of trivia, we moved with the masses up the wooded John Muir Trail, a pleasant, but sometimes rocky, path.

In 2005, yet another victim met his demise, voluntarily removing himself from the shallow end of the gene pool. A 24-year-old resident of San Francisco was swept over the edge of Vernal Fall after losing his balance and falling in the torrential current. Witnesses say the man ignored the many posted warning signs, in multiple languages (apparently, though, not written in *stupid*), then leapt over the guardrail near the precipice of the fall to wash his face and cool off in the river. Park rangers and rescue crews searched the Merced River below the 317 ft. cliff, but never found the body. *Never found the body!* Authorities listed the man as presumed dead. Really—do you think?

Yet, in the 80s, there went our little entourage, pressing forward on this L.A. freeway of a trail, onward and upward. I had our youngest riding me in a child backpack; my wife attempting to corral the two others. This was made all the more difficult in the throngs with Cary continuing to stop to try to feed the overly friendly squirrels small rocks for lunch. The rodents—plague-ridden, no doubt—would take the pebbles in their little hands with great expectation. You can imagine their disappointment.

It was about this time—sweating profusely—that I realized I probably hadn't brought enough water for everyone, but I kept that to myself for the time being. No reason to dampen spirits so early, less than a mile from the parking area. And with the sun beating down on us, I selfishly rationalized—as I downed another gulp—that as the pack mule, I might need more hydration than the others.

Fortunately, the crowds thinned out after the trail crossed a bridge. This is the first view of the spectacular Vernal Fall, and I guess enough for a lot of folks who choose not to trudge up the cliff side, switchback path to the top. And it's this juncture, I came to find out later, that is the recommended stopping point for those with small children. What was I thinking, when deciding to press on?

The trail forked, and we took the direction of the aptly named Mist Trail. This trail completes the 1,000 ft. elevation gain from the parking lot to the top as it climbs steeply up a cliff out of the valley close enough to the thunderous fall to be caught up in its own weather-maker. To call this trail "misty" is akin to calling a flash flood a trickle.

What started out as refreshing droplets soon turned into a full-force tempest the higher we went, something on the scale of

Tales from the Trails

an F4 Category hurricane. Torrents of waterfall rain thrashed us from above and from the side as the wind blew right towards us. You don't just get wet, you get jump-in-the-shower-with-all-your-clothes-on drenched. I wished I had brought those rain ponchos still back at camp with me.

I skated on slippery, moss-covered rocks and almost went down, back-packed child in tow. Through the deafening roar, Diane, water streaming down her face, yelled something garbled to me like, "What are we doing? Turn back now! You're crazy!" What I heard her say was, "Keep going! We can make it!" I was so proud of her. She could be my shipmate in any Nor'easter Perfect Storm.

The sun stabbed through the mist at times, creating rainbows that morphed and danced across the valley, a promise that we would not be flooded out and drown here. We held hands and slogged on.

In the last quarter mile or so, the trail got steeper and narrower. Carved stones created a granite staircase but didn't improve the footing. I was happy with our effort as we passed people who were clinging to the side of the cliff, irrationally afraid of heights, slick-as-snot rock and a deadly, screaming tumble through the mist to the boulders and whitewater below.

We broke through to welcome sunshine as the path opened onto a large, flat knob on top of Vernal Fall, with a railing to hold back the curious from going too close to the cliff edge overlooking the fall. We caught our breath and took in the beauty of our surroundings. Beyond the fall is a large, deceptively tranquil pond called Emerald Pool. More than a dozen tourists have died here in the last decade by entering at water's edge or by sliding down the Silver Apron slope at the far end, not realizing that strong undercurrents existed that may not be visible from the surface.

A rather dramatic warning sign showing a flailing, silhouette man about to be swept over the edge of the fall caught my attention. Text next to the illustration matter-of-factly stated: "Stay back from the water's edge. If you slip and go over the waterfall, you will die." I wanted to add, "...and your body will never be found."

Everywhere, families and friends sat to take in the sights, picnic, and rest before starting the descent to the parking area. Despite how many had turned back earlier, quite a few people surrounded the pool. In some ways, the Euro males sunbathing in Speedos were scarier than the waterfall. What is it about these guys wanting to wear nothing but tight undies out in public? Are they not aware that—

I was jolted out of my strange stream of consciousness by collective gasps and screams from the crowd. I looked around to see what the fuss was about, and saw a young boy hanging by his fingertips from the *other side* of the railing right next to the waterfall. He had clearly climbed over, or through, the railing, and his feet had slipped out from underneath him on the wet rail. From the back, the boy reminded me of our little soot-covered Cary.

A Good Samaritan grabbed the boy's wrist and pulled him back through the rail, onto solid ground. The man immediately looked around to find the parents who would let a small child run free on top of a 300 ft. waterfall. In fact, the whole crowd was now spying for the irresponsible parents, with a look like, "Who would do such a thing? What idiot parent would let this happen?"

Any loving parent who's had a child pull away from them in a grocery or department store, and had that moment of panic that the child was lost or stolen, would understand how fast this happens with kids. I felt a bit of empathy for these parents, so I looked around too, waiting for them to come forward. I thought this might be a good object lesson for Cary—

He had been right here! Just now! Next to me. We were looking for a spot to have trail snacks and dry out....

Realization hit me like a wall of water. The boy was Cary! I ran over to him—all eyes on me—choking back my own gasp and tears. I held my curious, adventurous son tightly: maybe I'd never let go of my hold. He told us he was just trying to get a better view. He didn't mean to scare us, or to slip; he just wanted to see what it was like to look right down a waterfall.

Eventually, the crowd grew bored of glaring at me and whispering to each other and went back to viewing the fall, the surrounding mountains, or the Euro males in Speedos. One *less* person went over Vernal Fall that year.

You may want to hear that Cary and I went on to live safe, careful lives, avoiding risk to this day, devoid of idiocy, but that wasn't the case. Such is the enjoyment for exploration in life, especially one lived with a love for the outdoors. Together we went on many more adventures. But those are other tales.

Life and Death in 12 Falls Canyon

Bailey Canyon, San Gabriel Mountains, California

*There are no seven wonders of the world
in the eyes of a child. There are seven million.*

— Walt Streightiff —

As canyons go, Bailey Canyon is not particularly special. The smallish canyon is just a short, rugged gap into the base of the San Gabriel Mountains in Southern California (one point of access to the Angeles Forest). But, as a kid, it had been a place brimming with possibilities for exploring. Its size had no limits on adventure for my friends and me.

Any evidence of pioneer history connected to the canyon had long since gone back to nature. Once, local trappers had snared fox and coyote along the foothills and shipped the pelts to furriers in Chicago. In 1875, R. J. Bailey homesteaded the canyon, and left nothing but his name.

My parents had built a typical 1960s, one-level stucco home in the small community of Sierra Madre, literally a friendly neighborhood block away from the Bailey Canyon trailhead. My friends and I considered this our own, private hiking and climbing canyon—and, in many ways it was. This was before it became popular, before it became the Bailey Canyon Wilderness Park, developed with a parking lot, public restrooms, a fire pit, picnic areas with barbeque grills, and surrounded by a groomed nature trail. My boyhood canyon was still *wild* wilderness.

Mine was an idyllic childhood, especially in the summertime. Those were simpler times before cable TV, text messaging, *Angry*

Tales from the Trails

*Bird*s, the multi-plex movie theater, the Wii, surfing the Internet, and on-line gaming. We actually got *outside*.

My buddies and I used to ride to each other's houses on our banana-seated Schwinn Sting-Ray bikes (with playing cards clothes-pinned to the spokes of the wheels for that cool, faux motorcycle sound). We built backyard tree forts. We trolled barefoot downtown alleyways for redeemable glass soda pop bottles, hoping to collect enough change to buy our own chilled beverage. We walked the aisles of Macabob's Toy Store, daydreaming of participating in some TV show contest where we would race around filling a shopping cart with as much merchandise as we could collect in 60 seconds. We climbed chain link fences by the Little League fields and swam across small reservoirs in our underwear. And we hiked the foothills.

One early summer day the buddies and I headed up to Bailey Canyon. It had been known by that name for some time, but we called it 12 Falls Canyon. We had hiked here before, but not so early in the morning, and not with this cloud cover. In Southern California, the weather forecasters called it "June Gloom." Moisture would gather over the Pacific Ocean the night before and roll in onshore up to the foothills, creating a dismal grayness that sometimes burned off by noon, sometimes just mixed with the smog for the rest of the day. We didn't care—the atmosphere added to the adventure.

We didn't really know if there actually were twelve distinct waterfalls in the drainage. Looking back now, I think that a legitimate waterfall would have to be something more than a trickle from a seasonal creek; a bit greater than a small stream spilling over a boulder. Our fat Webster's Dictionary at home would not define these spillways as waterfalls. But, hey, we were just kids. Someone had counted at one point—12 Falls it was called, and the nickname stuck for us.

At the trailhead, one of the guys questioned whether this was really a good idea that day. A bit of drizzle started falling. Discussion ensued as we chain locked our bikes together. Many of the waterfalls were steep, slick, worn granite that required sure footing even on a dry day. Our swimming hole would probably be all muddy. We debated the (unlikely) possibility of a flash flood. None of the issues dampened our enthusiasm as we chose to press forward up the trail that follows the streambed into the canyon.

The clouds had settled in on the foothills. Visibility was about as far as we could throw a Beatles 45 record. Familiar surroundings now looked ominous, clothed in the wet mist. A light breeze blew past us, leading our way. Tree branches seemed to reach out at our little group of explorers like skeletal specters; spiked willows grabbed at our denim pant legs in protest of our ascent. The fog obscured every aspect of the trail that now looked alien. This was not the happy lark of a hike that we had enjoyed other warm summer days.

The slippery rock spillways offered little traction. We hiked past (and counted) six of the falls, staying to the side of the stream, and avoiding the poison oak lurking along the trail. We had all heard the stories of "some neighborhood kid" that had transferred the oak's toxic sap (and eventually, the red, blistering, itchy rash) to "down there" when he touched "it" to pee. Whether anyone had really ever known someone to whom that had happened or not, none of us wanted to take a chance of *that* accidentally occurring.

The canyon became narrow and craggy. At some point we stopped counting waterfalls. We knew when we spied the *big* one, we would count it as the 12th fall. The waterfall was about 20 feet high, but seemed much larger from our young vantage point. This really was our destination, as climbing from this point on was very difficult and technical, nearly inaccessible.

As we rounded the final turn to our goal, the "smell of death" hit us like an invisible, putrid flash flood. I wouldn't have known the odor of decay, having never smelled it before. But, boy, did this stink! The closest I had ever been to death was frying ants on the sidewalk with a magnifying glass.

We were both fascinated and repulsed by what we saw. A good flow cascaded over the large fall. More water than usual splashed up from the rocks at its base. A large buck lay across boulders about 30 feet downstream, soaked from the spray of the waterfall and rain. The stench was so strong we tried to cover our noses, and one of my buddies later said he thought he was going to blow chunks.

A silence hung over our group like the fog on the foothills. In these frozen moments, even the low roar of the waterfall seemed hushed. We stared in disbelief. The deer gaped blankly back.

"He must have fallen ... from up there," someone finally said, pointing up the cliff wall. "Slipped at the edge, and came crashing down."

Just an accident. Full of life at one moment. Gone the next. A slip on gravel, a miscalculation of distance, or not knowing if the ground was solid enough to support its weight, and, in a micro-second, it was all over. Our young minds didn't go all philosophical about the shortness or seeming capriciousness of life. We just wanted to poke the deer with a stick.

Being curious boys, of course we had to give this a detailed examination. We deduced from the lack of serious rigor mortis (from analytical stick poking) that this incident had not happened that long ago. We walked around it and could see no obvious cause for its death, other than the fall. No hunter had shot it at cliff's edge. A creature so sure footed had just made a mistake, we deduced.

Nature has a way of taking care of its own—its fallen are recycled. When we came back months later, most evidence of the deer's demise was gone, except for a few bleached bone fragments. The body had gone back to the land, its home, one way or another.

○ ○ ○

Flash forward some 20 years, and here I was with Diane and my kids, Sarah, Cary, and Daniel, exploring the same Bailey Canyon, trying to count 12 waterfalls. We had been up the canyon a number of times—one of our favorite "local" hikes. It was close to our home, now a couple of communities away from my boyhood neighborhood, and still a welcome, convenient getaway from the urban sprawl of the Greater Los Angeles landscape.

I shared with the kids my love for the canyon that began many years earlier when I was a child full of wonder about the natural world. I told of the deer story and other canyon escapades. Diane and I hoped this hot, summer day would bring such similar adventures for our little ones and us—well, maybe without a deer carcass. Wildflowers and thick-trunked oaks greeted us at the trailhead. The tree branches housed a myriad of chirping greeters.

The canyon now seemed smaller to me, less wild, and the *big* waterfall not nearly as tall as I remembered. But this was the kids' time of exploration, and each turn in the trail yielded a new wonder, a fresh opportunity to discover, or a surprise: the explosion and celebration of life in nature.

Chuck Swindoll writes, "Each day of our lives we make deposits in the memory banks of our children." Of course, we hope these are good memories, even if it is a positive outcome from difficult circumstances.

Our grown kids still remember hiking "12 Falls Canyon," and it was still a wild wilderness to them. They remember that as the yawn in the foothills narrowed, the cliffs rose steeply, ruggedly, casting dark shadows over our path. They remember the big fall, water splashing down on worn rocks, creating a refreshing mist, and our climb around it to hike deeper into uncharted territory. They remember shedding their clothes to their undies and jumping into a cool swimming hole, laughing and splashing. Carefree.

Maybe they will take their kids there one day, recalling their own keen memories of their times there. Their memories, however, seem to have gained compounded interest: They remember counting 13 waterfalls.

One (Breathless) Step at a Time!

Quandary Peak, Tenmile Range, Colorado

"Men go back to the mountains, as they go back to sailing ships at sea, because in the mountains and on the sea they must face up, as did men of another age, to the challenge of nature ... in the hills and on the water the character of a man comes out."

— Abram T. Collier —

While I was climbing Colorado fourteeners and checking them off my list, I was often asked by those interested in a first-time climb, "What's an easy fourteener to start with?" I want to shout, "They are 14,000 ft. peaks—what are you expecting? They are mammoth, rugged, rocky mountains, with at least a 3,000 ft. elevation gain from the trailheads! This is no walk in the park!"

The polite answer is there are no easy ones. There are *easier* ones than others, but they are all tough. That being said, comparatively, Quandary Peak is an easier mountain to climb than some, but still long and challenging in its own way.

It's expected with just about everybody who climbs fourteeners—except for some of these human-mountain-goat-hybrid types—that at the higher elevations everyone takes a breathing break every ten paces or so. At high altitude, you simply have to. Your cells are screaming for you to stop at an oxygen bar. The higher up you go, normal breathing becomes heavy and labored, then panting, and eventually out and out gasping for air and wondering why you even do this.

I've taken several first-timers up fourteeners. I enjoy taking new people up, even if it's a peak I've summited before. The climb is fresh again for me viewed through their eyes. And I get to experience their heaving, complaining, and sometimes even their retching (which isn't exactly unexpected when altitude sickness combines with sheer exhaustion).

I've gotten everyone up the mountain, and back down again, in one piece. If not, I guess this would be a different type of book, something along the lines of a Donner Party story of survival. I wouldn't be trusted, or able, to take any other folks up the peaks, especially if I were in prison.

While it's expected that frequent breaks will be needed to catch your breath, to continue your momentum and pace (early start, summit and off the top of the mountain by noon to avoid the predictable afternoon summer thunder storms) stops must be short and standing. Lying down for long periods of time, unable to move or speak, is not going to hold the timetable. Such was the climb up Quandary with my nephew, Shawn O'Donnell.

My son, Cary, his cousin, Shawn, and I drove out to the trailhead the night before. We set up a tent, cooked a little dinner on our propane stove, and played some poker for granola and M & M's. Cary had climbed other peaks with me, so he knew the routine—up before dawn to start our ascent. But both teen boys were pretty excited about the next day's adventure, Shawn's first fourteener. It took them a long while to settle down in their mummy bags. By the way, lack of sleep the night before is a poor down payment toward your success on a fourteener the next day.

At 5:00 am when the travel alarm went off, their enthusiasm had dropped considerably. Were these the same boys from the (short) night before? I would have had an easier time rousing a log to get up and get going. Finally, after the offer of some orange juice and breakfast bars and the threat of covering them with honey and summoning fire ants to the picnic, we were all up and dressed with packs ready for hitting the trail—about an hour later than projected.

Quandary sits in the Tenmile Range as the reigning monarch, surrounded by lesser peaks rising in concert toward Quandary, with each reaching higher than the last. It is a good starter peak or early spring conditioning peak for the seasoned climber. Breaking out of the forest, from the tree line at 11,700 feet, there is a nice trail up gentle slopes for two miles to the summit.

For a first-timer, Shawn did very well ... for the first ten minutes or so. The need for oxygen and/or drink breaks quickly became more and more frequent. Standing breaks became sitting breaks. Sitting breaks turned to lying down breaks. After a while, lying down breaks required looking for a pulse. Minutes turned to hours, hours turned to, well, a lot more hours.

To his defense and credit, Shawn had come to visit with the family in Colorado from the lowlands of Maryland. Add to that a sedate life style and some left over pounds of baby fat. But he refused to quit—not that I ever gave him the option. We *were* going to make the top.

Cary and I made a good team to move Shawn step-by-step up the mountain. I tried to persuade, nag, cajole, urge, pester, threaten, and cheerlead him one foot after another. Shawn's participation in the partnership was to roll on the ground and moan for a while. I knew the peak summit was too much to ask all at once, so I tried to see if he could just get up and move to that next large boulder or stack of rocks 30 feet up. Just 10 yards at a time, and then another 10 yards (or five), we moved at a snail's pace up the long rising ridge. He wasn't going to give up, and neither was I. Cary continued to encourage Shawn all the way up as well. What should have taken about three to four hours, took around seven, but we made it.

When you reach the top of a fourteener, there's a kind of elation that is hard to describe. Typically upon reaching the summit, there are congratulations, manly hugs, a sense of camaraderie, and a real time of revelry as the high altitude panorama is scanned and the route accomplishment assessed as unbelievable. Our celebration was no exception. This sense of pride and triumph for a job well done is all the more accentuated if one didn't believe he could really make it. All the impossible hard work, pain and struggle to get to the top evaporates.

As Shawn turned slowly to try to absorb all the breath taking views, he was so proud of his success that he couldn't stop thanking me for helping him make it up. Seeing his joy and satisfaction was worth the effort. He couldn't wait to get down to the valley and call his mom to tell her what he was able to do. Shawn met a challenge, did a lot more than he thought he could ever accomplish, and showed his real character. He now knew for certain he was not one to give up in the face of difficulty. The victory made struggle worthwhile.

Spires, Surprises and Smelly Boys

Ansel Adams Wilderness, Sierra Nevada, California

"Somebody new always comes along and changes my mind about who I think I really like."

— Author Unknown —

N**umber One:** I don't care for backpacking. I don't like "sleeping" on rocks (those camping sleeping pads are useless) and freezing all night long (mummy bags just leave me cold). Lying awake, shivering, on hard ground, under the vast canopy of stars is just not my thing (and there are way too many stars, making me feel way too small).

I'm not fond of having to carry 70 pounds of dead weight in an uncomfortable backpack for miles, and I hate cleaning dirty camp dishes after a late-night meal, totally exhausted after the long day out. I don't like monster boot blisters, sore pack strap shoulders, the threat of hungry predators, freeze-dried dinners, iodine water purifiers, or swarms of blood-bloated mosquitoes the size of footballs.

Number Two: I don't really care much for teenage boys, despite, or because of, my wife and I having raised three ourselves. They can be annoying, exasperating, arrogant know-it-alls, disrespectful, argumentative, with attitude, reckless, messy, smelly, hyper and loud. Just like I was at their age.

In light of the above, it may seem incongruous, then, that I agreed (even volunteered) to go on a ten-day backpacking trip in the High Sierra with fifty loud, smelly, annoying teenage boys. But I wasn't going to miss a chance to get an all-expense-paid hiking trip to the Ansel Adams Wilderness (originally established as the Minarets Wilderness) in California, adjacent to Yosemite National Park. I'd survived many tough and scary wilderness challenges, so certainly I could endure this outdoor experience for the opportunity to trek through such a beautiful, wondrous area—one that I'd never hiked in before.

The author enjoying the Sierras, having momentarily stepped away from the smelly boys.

T. Duren Jones

Our ordeal, er, adventure, began at a hotel in Fresno the night before we hit the trail, which was about a two hour drive away. The boys were shuttled in vans from the airport from all around the country to the hotel. Those who gathered with roiling anticipation, trepidation, teenage angst and boisterous behavior were your stereotypical cast of high school characters: the fat kid, the bully, couch potato video game players, the outdoorsman, the out-of-shape asthmatic, the chess club or band nerds, the angry-at-the-world-and-everyone-in-it kid, the farmer's son, the "misunderstood" hardened juvenile delinquent with thick beard stubble (the 6-year high school student), the church kids, and variations in between featuring diverse levels of maturity, or complete lack thereof.

Most of these fifty boys—some as young as a tender thirteen, some pushing nineteen—looked forward to a physically challenging and character-testing outdoor event. Some attended reluctantly, their parents hoping for a tough week-and-a half rehabilitation experience for the boys, the rebellion hiked out of them. Whatever reason drew them here, they were now all committed to the expedition and adventures ahead of them.

I was able to attend as a staff member of a magazine directed to teen boys. This was the second year they had sponsored a High Sierras adventure trip. Five of us "counselors" plus three partner organization staff were responsible for these young lives for the week and a half in the rugged wilderness. After the first evening, I was ready to leave some in the mountains.

The no-running-and-shouting-in-the-hotel-hallways rule was immediately ignored. Apparently high on vending machine sodas and candy bars (and with the euphoria of no parental guidance), any respectable home behavior was tossed out the second story window. Miles of tromping through the woods with heavy backpacks would expend some of this excess energy.

The evening before our start we were all called together for a team spirit time and explanation of what we could expect for the next several days. After a fine dinner of real food—the last we would have for a while—we gathered in the hotel conference room to meet and break up into our teams (ten teens per leader). Following the welcome, brief speaker presentations, much cheerleading and other associated hoopla, we broke into our "tribes." Our task was to come up with a tribe name, a warrior symbol and motto or theme song, if we were so inclined. The testosterone cloud in the room was thick.

I was hoping to have a group of guys who, together, would come up with a manly tribal name and icon like Swift Antelope, Snarling Bear, Howling Wolf, Leaping Cougar, Bloody Spear, Snapping Turtle, and the like. As an outdoorsman, and an artist, I tingled with anticipation at the possibilities, and my imagination raced at thoughts of our new collective tribal identity and face paint. We were given timeframe and poster paint was handed out.

How was it possible that by some random selection I was grouped with *all* the tech geeks? Instead of choosing a name like Charging Moose, they unanimously selected the mathematical number pi, with the $\prod$ symbol to be drawn on our faces and a warrior chant involving 3.14159.

I looked around the room and could see the other tribes face painting symbols for Angry Dog, Clawing Eagle, and Stampeding Buffalo. You can imagine my disappointment and consternation at having to explain how my historical Indian tribe even knew about complex mathematical concepts.

Each tribe presented its identity to the others, whooped and hollered around an imagined fire pit, and worked itself up into a frenzy that I'm sure was not conducive to a good night's sleep. I was a good sport, joining the festivities, secretly fighting the urge to find a seat in the back row and disappear.

The next morning came way too early for most, especially for those fueled by sugar highs and aggressively-named tribal pride. We loaded up and drove our 15-passenger vans to the outdoors expedition partnership organization I shall call "Purposeful Adventures in Nature" to protect the guilty, AKA PAIN for reasons that will become evident. To say that these guys were nature conscious would be an understatement. I'm all for protecting our treasured natural resources and caring for the wilderness. But these hard-core environmentalists made the Sierra Club look like pansies.

The PAIN representatives gave us an overview of the ten days to come: miles of hiking, camping, map use, orienteering and path finding, meal prep and clean up, mountain climbing, rope work, rappelling, etc. (They did save some surprises for us.) They went over the wilderness rules of conduct and etiquette—all generally accepted behavior for the responsible outdoorsman, and the extra emphasis probably good for the boys. But these extreme "tree-huggers" added a few regulations of their own.

The "leave no trace" policy is a wise one for wilderness experiences. As good stewards of wild and open spaces, we should care for our natural resources, and prepare for a great time for those who follow us by leaving our camp pristine. But the PAIN staff took it to absurd levels.

We learned that we would all share in the cooking and clean up. We would all police the camp for any trash. Fine, I'm onboard so far.

No food scraps, of any kind, would be left behind. Period. Any spilled food particles were to be picked up—and they meant every last morsel. I had always thought a few breadcrumbs left for Sammy Squirrel would be an unexpected and much appreciated treat. Boy, was I wrong!

We were to leave no reason for any woodland creature to leave its natural diet and come into vacated camps for snacks. Because some locations may be frequented as camps, no animal should come to depend on scraps for sustenance. Poor guys. I've seen how hard an ant works to take one tasty find back to his buddies.

In addition, fire pit ashes were to be buried, rocks used for pit and seating would be randomly redistributed around "camp," and the grounds were to be swept with pine branches to erase foot and pad impressions. Wow, Old West frontier scouts would never have been able to find our route.

We also learned what would go into our packs, and how to pack them for good weight distribution—apparently creating balance, just like for pack mules. In addition to the individual necessities (sleeping bag, pad, camera, jacket, gloves, etc.) each of us would be required to carry the divided and packaged food for the 10 days ... bringing the combined weight to just about 75 pounds per pack. I didn't remember reading that in the promotional brochure. I thought we'd be using Himalayan Sherpas, or someone, to carry our gear.

At that time, the weight of the pack would have been about half my body mass! And with some of the younger teens, this would have been the equivalent of carrying another person of similar size on their backs. In addition, each day several hikers would "volunteer" to carry the heavy climbing ropes, adding around 15 more pounds to their packs for that day.

The PAIN staff had to show us how to load the packs without any help, a combination of strategic technique and brute strength. It started with a kind of standing squat, legs spread, then throwing the pack up to one knee, followed by struggling one arm at a time through the straps. With a "you've got to be kidding me" expression, the first time I hoisted the hippo-sized pack on my back, my legs almost buckled, trembled wildly, and I could barely keep my balance. I thought with my first step I'd topple over. If I went down backwards, arms and legs flailing skywards, I'd have to be rolled over like a turtle on its back.

The next bit of instruction from our nature drill sergeants solicited hoots, hollers, giggles, belly laughs, crude comments and body noises expected from a crowd of teen guys. If a discussion of outdoor potty practices makes you uncomfortable, perhaps you should jump ahead to the next section. This is, of course, a natural act for all of us, but one less convenient in the wilderness, and slightly more complicated if we want to leave the outdoors just as we found it.

We were told that responsibly taking care of your "business" required that you "go" a couple dozen yards outside the camp perimeter (no makeshift camp privies were constructed) and even farther away from any creeks or lakes. We needed to dig a "cat hole" to make a deposit, bury the evidence, and cover the dirt mound with a rock, fallen pine branches and/or scattered leaves and pine needles. We were all to comply, no exceptions, but I'm not sure who would be policing the cheaters.

Then, here's the part that really got everyone's attention, and had me add extreme environmentalists to my dislike list: no toilet paper would be allowed. For a 10-day backpacking trip? Seriously? I had signed up for a lot, but not for this! I had phantom chaffing just at the thought of this! Isn't T. P. one of the things that separate us from the animal world? (That, along with opposable thumbs, and not smelling each other's rear ends for a greeting.)

Natural alternatives were generously offered by the PAIN staff (not necessarily in any tush-friendliness order). One could use a handful of dry leaves (uncomfortable groans emanated from the crowd). Green pine needles, delicately used in the right direction (double uncomfortable groans). Tree bark, carefully (guffaws). A smooth streambed stone, preferably wet (bursts of laughter). And the PAIN staff added suggestions of moss, leaves (no poison ivy), snow, grasses, smooth sticks, and pine cones, not open (roll in the aisles hilarity followed).

Someone shouted from the audience just to use your hand, with splashed bottled water (more groans again). The idea being a sort of wilderness French bidet, I guess. Someone else shouted back that they hoped that person wasn't making dinner that night!

The most appealing natural toilet paper alternative for most was the final suggestion: where they could be found, select a few, fresh broad, open leaves located by many creek banks. These were large enough, soft enough, durable enough, and relatively painless to do the duty. When we stopped to cross a stream, and those plants were available, each hiker would be allowed to take and pack up to five leaves for future use. I was less than thrilled with any of the alternatives; especially putting a leaf I knew nothing about down *there*.

The only exception to the rule is that we could bring T. P. as long as we carried it out with us. Clinging to a necessary creature comfort, and my last shred of humanity, I chose this option. I had gotten a heads-up from one of our counselors who had attended the previous year, so I came prepared. If I put baking soda, mixed with baby powder in a one-gallon sealable plastic bag to hold the used T.P., this alternative seemed doable. I had, after all, helped my wife raise four kids, so this couldn't be any worse than the diaper pail we had used. I would make this work.

○ ○ ○

The PAIN staff wanted to get some miles behind us the first day. We lugged our stuffed packs into pickups and vans and took off. At the trailhead, we said our goodbyes to civilization (and most, also to T.P.) and immediately started up a steep ascent through thick woods.

My ridiculously heavy pack felt like the laws of gravity had changed, compressing me closer to the center of earth. I depended a lot on my hiking stick for stability and propulsion—the boys called it my cane because of its handle top. Still, I was kind of proud of myself, as I held my own about in the middle of the pack.

No bets were placed, but many were wondering whether the asthmatic, out-of-shape Floridian would make it through the first day, let alone the entire ten days. There were pullout points should there be any emergencies. Sure enough, he was down before the second uphill mile.

The young, bespeckled lad had not wanted to come on this trip, didn't think he could make it in the wilderness, but forced by his mother, here he lay on his back in the middle of the rocky trail. Whether due to the higher altitude, poor conditioning, shortness of breath, dehydration, lack of sleep, or some combination of the above, our sea-level flatlander moaned in the dust, surrounded by curious gawking teen companions.

We sat him up, hydrated the poor fellow, forced a Snickers bar down him, and after a while, asked him if he thought he could continue, or needed to go back to the trailhead. Much to our surprise, he perked up, and with character, grit and determination, he was insistent that he be allowed to continue, and that he could make the whole trip. We lightened his load a bit for the first day, several boys offering to carry the extra weight for him. All the teens came around him to cheer him on. Even the *supposed* bully patted him on the back.

Day after day, we marched on, exploring mile after mile of pristine, wondrous backcountry. We slept under the stars, in crisp, cool, thin air, open to the elements, with no tents. Thunderstorms and afternoon and evening rain showers are not as common to the High Sierra as they are predictably in the Rockies.

The Ansel Adams Wilderness is a wild area of over 231,000 acres, bordering Yosemite National Park. The region used to be called the Minarets Wilderness, named for the centerpiece jagged ridge of peaks considered one of the most spectacular massifs in the Sierra. The area was enlarged in 1984 by the California Wilderness Act, and the name was changed to Ansel Adams, honoring the famous landscape photographer and environmentalist. 349 miles of trails traverse portions of the wilderness and include the John Muir Trail and the Pacific Crest Trail.

The personalities of the teens seemed to grow larger in this expanse. The loud ones got even louder; singing improvised silly songs at the top of their lungs, over and over again, nearly ruining the outdoor experience for those who wanted simply to enjoy the sounds of solitary wilderness silence. The bully, goofing around, *accidentally* broke someone's expensive hiking stick, making his earlier altruistic act of kindness to the asthmatic seem suspect. The nerds, and the outdoorsmen, knew everything (academically or experientially) about the wilderness trail finding, map reading and orienteering, geology, mineral content, star constellations, eatable wild berries, and big leaf toilet paper, and ceaselessly shared all that information with others.

One deeply troubled—and trouble-making—young man spiraled down to a dark place. It wasn't until a few days into the trip that he shared that he had recently lost his father. He was angry at life, at death, at God, the world, and everybody in it. It was no wonder he was acting up so much. It was gratifying for me to see the PAIN staff, our publication staff counselors, and even some other boys, rally alongside him to offer non-judgmental understanding and comfort. Whether we wanted to or not, we were developing a bond among us all. What a concept.

I made a trail buddy along the way with one teen, and we spent a lot of time together. Initially, he was put off by the goof-offs, loud mouths and troublemakers. I guess we shared the same responses to what stood in such opposition to the wilderness experience. A senior, he loved the outdoors like I did, had a maturity beyond his age, could discuss the important things in life, was goal-driven, and simply a delight to share these natural wonders with. I really liked this guy (a teen!), and he restored my faith in this upcoming generation.

The PAIN leadership team of our expedition proved to live up to their credo. They were serious, but wanted to have (safe) fun too. They were knowledgeable and experienced, but rigid in their instruction, providing education and safety for a variety of outdoor activities including long-distance hiking, backpacking, high-altitude camping, mountaineering, climbing and rappelling and other rope work (even pulling ourselves from cliff edge to cliff edge over a roaring river!).

And they did live up to their "leave no trace" philosophy and practice. Camps were left as we found them, or better, on durable surfaces. If one could sleep on a rock slab rather than the dirt above tree line, all the better. Of course, the smallest bit of trash debris was picked up, and any meal prep or cleanup spills were immediately taken care of.

Wouldn't you know it, right on my turn to assist with dinner, in the dark, except for headlamps, I spilled half a pot of cooked rice—all to collective gasps, and my shame. We saved what we could for the meal, and the rest I was assigned to pick up grain by grain, and dispose of properly. Talk about obsessive! And committed. One day, at lunchtime, I saw a PAIN leader, on all fours, sucking spilled jelly off a large rock. That was an image that will stay with me a long time.

I survived the 10 days backpacking in the high country with 50 teen boys. And, surprisingly, I enjoyed most of it. We covered about 60 miles, climbing up and down rugged mountains via high passes, traversing across open wild-flowered meadows, negotiating rushing streams and pushing through lush, deep woods. We even trudged through late-season snow.

We endured sleepless nights, blistered feet, aching shoulders, and cold mornings venturing out of our mummy bags. We suffered through stupid hiking songs, sometimes loutish, youthful behavior, swarms of blood-thirsty mosquitos, sunburn, rope burns, freeze-dried meals, backpacking body odor, wilderness potty etiquette, and challenges beyond what any of us thought we could do. But I wouldn't have traded the memories of this trip for anything.

I frequently reminisce about jumping into an ice-cold alpine lake for a bracing bird bath, our good late-night campfire talks, helping (and trusting) each other through difficult exercises like blindfolded cliff climbing and rappelling, our first view of the Minaret spires across a snowfield, afternoon light dancing off a pond by our campsite, with reeds swaying in a breeze, and, most importantly, seeing, with joy, genuinely changed lives. No one comes away from an experience like this unaffected.

○ ○ ○

Epilog: My Pi tribe melded well into the collective, becoming one cohesive, supportive, mobile community. The heavy kid shed some pounds that he committed to keep off. The couch potatoes got in shape, and thought it was pretty cool to be outside and away from video games. The urban and farm teens got a better understanding of each other's culture. The nerds weren't so weird after all, in fact, aside from their quirkiness, or because of it, they were downright interesting, and entertaining. The bully's need for attention, he found, was better served, and better received, through acts of kindness.

My young trail buddy and I stayed in contact as he entered college, broke up with his long-time girlfriend, solo canoed a good portion of Michigan's Upper Peninsula, and really found his legs to a good start in life. That next summer, he flew out to Colorado to stay with my family a few days, and we summited a 14er together with friends.

The teen who had so recently suffered such loss found some healing, and I believe made peace with his circumstances, his emptiness, and his maker. We watched the anger stripped away like a shed coat in the warm sun.

I went on this backpacking adventure for selfish reasons, I admit. I wanted to see some beautiful wilderness, and have some new experiences. I also wanted to have some influence on these teen boys, and see some changed lives. I came away, surprised that, perhaps, I had changed the most.

These teen guys were great, and gave me confidence that with young people like these, there is a hope for the future of our world. I came to genuinely like, and certainly respect the PAIN staff, despite what they put us all through. I found that either in building relationships, or in rugged mountain challenges, I could do more than I imagined.

I'm becoming cautiously more enthusiastic about backpacking. Just a bit. And through experiences like this, I've really come to appreciate a few of the little things in life. Things like a comfortable bed, a pillow, a warm shower, toilet paper, flushing toilets, paper towels, escalators....

Lost Canyons and Large Toilet Bowls

Needles District, Canyonlands National Park, Utah

*"The high desert has an effect on people.
The place has a way of swallowing you up."*

— Campbell Scott —

Imagine trudging endlessly through miles of sand with big hiking boots. Picture yourself carrying a heavy pack on an unseasonably warm, fall day. Think about a wide, shallow creek that keeps intersecting your way and you decide it's just easier to splash through it than to keep stopping to remove your boots. Now, imagine hours of this.

This is not Marine Corps training on the Pacific Ocean beach at Camp Pendleton. This was the desert canyon trail I choose to trek in the Needles District in Canyonlands. No kidding. I actually chose to do this. No one held a rattlesnake to my head.

Such was the "trail" leaving the parking area in this section of the Needles District. One book even offered the advice, "Beware of quicksand." Great. As if I didn't have enough challenges already. Would I recognize it if I saw it? Did I even know how to get out of quicksand, should I find myself waist-deep in such a predicament? Lie flat and swim on top, or something, I remembered from some old Tarzan movie. But this was the desert, not the jungle. Still, I stayed alert for quagmires, and alligators.

The Salt Creek Trail is really nothing more than a broad sandy wash leading to Horse Canyon. The long slog to my destination of a natural arch named Paul Bunyan's Potty—no giggling, please—was beautiful, but seemed to offer no solid footing. I would have done better with snowshoes on, but that doesn't seem appropriate in the desert.

This hike had been on my bucket (sand pail?) list, but I was beginning to have second thoughts. I wondered if the hard work would be worth it.

My first treat was a short side trip to white and red picto-graphs at Peekaboo Springs. I'm not making up these names. Ancestral Pueblo people created this delicate rock artwork of turtles or shields or an ancient woman's new Bedrock Department Store purse (so it looked to me), perhaps some 1,300 years ago. I thought that even with my limited artistic skills I could have done better, but, hey, I'm no art critic.

By the way, I would recommend *not* taking the wrong turn to the aptly named Lost Canyon, like I did, adding time and extra mileage. While in Lost Canyon, I didn't really feel like I was lost until I was, well, lost. A simple trail sign announcing this forlorn area might keep hikers from unwarily wandering in, and never returning. Lacking any breadcrumbs, I carefully retraced my steps, trying not to confuse them with what must have been other lost souls and finally got back to my sandy trail. Miles of sand never looked so good as I pressed on.

I pushed through the sandy dry creek bed wondering if I might be better off removing my boots and walking barefoot, like on a beach. I left the boots on not wanting my tender, pink flesh to accidentally uncover something intent on poking, biting or stinging me. I considered cutting corners on this serpentine route to save time and effort, but the possibility of rattlesnake or cactus on slightly higher ground discouraged that. After what seemed like hours, I reached my destination.

Paul Bunyan's Potty (yes, the arch really looks like a giant toilet, but from the bottom of the bowl point of view) was remarkable. Yet, it made me uncomfortable at the same time. I'm sorry, but the stains leaking down from the sandstone just added to the impression. Nature never ceases to amaze with its splendor and variety. Something can be beautiful and disturbing at the same time.

I decided to press on a bit further through my own little Sahara Desert. My literature spoke of what became the real delight of the hike: Tower Ruin. I rounded an interminable number of curves and I came upon the cliff dwelling. What a great stop! The abode was impossibly built into a precipice that over-looks a broad, grassy park surrounded by sheer sandstone walls. I climbed up as close as I dared, and could see some roof beams still in place, held by the primitively placed rock walls. A nice little cave apartment with a view.

The march back the same trail was equally exhausting, but had I quit early on, as I was tempted due to the difficulty, wet boots and poor trail finding, I would have missed some spectacular sights. I'm glad I made the extra effort. Yet...something about Paul Bunyan's Potty still haunts me. I'll try to flush the discomfort from my mind.

Grin and Bear It

Culebra Peak, Sangre de Cristo Range, Colorado

"Wilderness can be defined as a place where humans enjoy the opportunity of being attacked by a wild animal."

— Edward Abby —

Knowing I enjoy hiking in remote wilderness areas, a friend sent me this important notice:
"The Montana State Department of Fish and Game is advising hikers, hunters, and fishermen to take extra precautions and keep alert for bears while in wilderness regions. People are advised to wear noise-producing devices such as little bells on their clothing to alert but not startle a bear. They advise carrying pepper spray in case of an encounter with a bear. It is also a good idea to watch for fresh signs of bear activity and know the difference between black and grizzly bear droppings. Black bear droppings are smaller and contain berries and possibly squirrel fur. Grizzly bear droppings have little bells in them and smell like pepper spray."

Although this humorous warning is of dubious origin, its advice about looking for signs and the benefits of good preparation are points well taken. On the trail, knowing how to come prepared for any situation can make the difference between arriving home for dinner and being dinner. (Even though many outdoor books do recommend wearing bells on your shoes or pack when in bear country, that always just seemed like ringing a supper bell to me, so I've avoided it.)

This life lesson became very apparent to me at about 13,000 feet on Culebra Peak. This southernmost 14,000 ft. mountain in Colorado is only nine miles from the New Mexico border. The name means "harmless snake" in Spanish, perhaps acquiring its name because of its gentle nature and long, winding northwest ridge.

In my years of hiking the Rockies I had seen plenty of wildlife—badgers, black bears, elk, porcupines, moose, bighorn sheep, coyotes and deranged, dive-bombing crows. All could do me harm if they wanted, I suppose. But most wildlife, with perhaps the exception of mountain lions, mind their own business and keep their distance from humans. And I keep my distance from them.

We don't have grizzly bears that we know of in Colorado. I have encountered black bears several times. Once I was hiking with my then six-year-old son, Spencer. We had just been discussing what to do if we came upon a bear or a cougar in the wilderness. We turned a bend in the trail and there was a mother bear and two cubs on the other side of a small creek. We backed up, talking, not making eye contact; the bears went on their own way, apparently seeing us as no threat. Living in close proximity to Pike National Forest, we had even found a black bear in our garage one night knocking over our trashcans in search of some smelly refuse to eat (no, not the first drafts of this book). But I had never seen a bear on any of my Colorado fourteener climbs.

I was climbing Culebra Peak with special permission (the mountain and the land around it for miles are all on a privately owned ranch) with Kevin. We were on a charity climb and he was writing an article for a Denver newspaper. I was his photographer. Coming up on part of the faint trail that leveled out for a few hundred yards, I noticed a shape that was something *different* from the scattered boulders—and it was moving. Typically, this is unusual behavior for a large rock.

We pulled out our field glasses and sure enough, a large black bear was fixed at attention, looking intently at us (without binoculars). We hadn't seen any bear droppings giving us warning and hadn't worn any bells. The bear stood right in our path, and had little motivation to move. This put us in a bit of a quandary. We had worked fairly hard to get permission for this climb and were not about to turn back. Both sides of the saddle dropped off steeply, so "bear ridge" was our only choice.

Although *Ursus Americanus* are smaller than grizzlies and lack their cousin's unpleasant disposition, they still can be a formidable presence. The black bear can grow up to 7 feet from nose to short tail and may weigh up to 600 pounds. Lean bears can exceed speeds of 30 mph—and can both run uphill and downhill. If you are being chased, hope that your pursuer is an old, fat bear in a winter coat who overheats and tires quickly.

The black bear has built-in crampons—non-retractable 2-inch claws on all four feet, allowing it to open logs in search of tasty treats or to climb trees rapidly. A black bear can scramble up a 100 ft. oak in 30 seconds. And did I mention they are omnivores? Knowing all this, as our bear took a couple of steps toward us, we had reasonable cause for concern, and took a few steps backwards.

I unholstered my canister of pepper spray that was about the size of a small fire extinguisher. We determined that if we were going to have a bear encounter, we'd better know how to use this thing—something, we realized, we should have practiced at home and not field tested with our target moving towards us.

"Quick," Kevin said, "let's read the instructions!" This required me to dig for my reading glasses because the print had to be small enough for all the dangers and disclaimers to fit on the can label. We knew the contents should be kept away from children (and was not to be used on unruly children), should not be ingested internally (really?), nor used close to an open flame—we were just trying to figure out how to get the darn protective cap off.

"We should give it a try," I suggested. Arms extended, and with some trepidation, I squeezed the trigger. A thick spray shot out for about four yards. I was surprised at how concentrated it stayed for so many feet.

"Wind!" we both yelled as a good amount of the brown amorphous fog changed direction, blowing right back toward us.

We stumbled back over rocks, turned our heads away, and got just a whiff of the vile contents. We could see how giving a bear or mountain lion a muzzle full of the spray could very well deter it from chomping down on us. Our stinging eyes filled with tears and we began to laugh hard between our coughing. For a moment forgetting we had real, not hypothetical, bear issues to deal with.

Maybe the whole pepper spray thing was a bad idea from the start. Now, not only were we salty with sweat from our steep ascent to this ridge, but our soft, rare flesh was seasoned with pepper. All that was needed was rice and veggies on the side to complete this tasty meal we'd created.

Looking back at our adversary, we watched as he waddled down a grassy descent in the direction of the forest below, either bored by the standoff, or satisfied that we were too stupid to be any threat to him. I thought I heard him roaring with laughter as he disappeared down the hill.

I guess I learned that with bear spray it's imperative to read the directions and the warnings (we must have rushed through the "do not spray into the wind" part). And I was reminded to be ready *before* I encounter any challenging situations. We bear-ly avoided being a high alpine picnic treat. I'd be better *prepared* in the future—wait, maybe that's not the right word.

The Start with a Finish

Colorado Trail, Beginning and End, Denver to Durango

"My therapist told me the way to achieve true inner peace is to finish what I start. So far today, I have finished 2 bags of M&M's and a chocolate cake. I feel much better."

— Dave Barry —

It's a story covering 486 miles, most of it at an elevation above 10,000 feet, and it took us years to complete. It is divided up into 28 segments, and is a tale that we will tell, in part, over and over again. The challenge took Kevin, Diane and me trekking from Denver to Durango, passing through eight mountain ranges, six National Forests, six designated wilderness areas, along five river systems, and through what is considered to be some of Colorado's most beautiful country. You can't see this wondrous landscape from your car—if you could, it sure would have been a lot easier.

I'm not sure what drove us to want to complete the Colorado Trail from end to end. Perhaps our love for the outdoors, especially the wild places. Maybe it was due to the fact that Kevin and I had summited *all* the 54 Colorado Fourteeners and were looking for a new quest, and another list to check off. (We were going through 14er withdrawals.) Or it could have been that, at certain places, our 14er climbing trails shared small portions with the Colorado Trial (CT), and we were simply intrigued to see the rest. Probably all of the above.

In any case, we started hiking, and we hiked, and hiked the nearly 500 rugged miles, breaking the total length into bite-sized pieces. We had too many adventures to tell in one sitting, but most stories have a beginning and an end. Here's ours:

Tales from the Trails

The Beginning

Maybe Kevin, Diane, and I were just too excited. Giddy, really. In our enthusiasm to start hiking the CT, we probably began the first section too early in the season. By the end of April most of the snow along the foothills of the eastern Front Range had melted away. We thought we might encounter some snow patches on the north side of shaded forests, but weren't too worried. We were anxious to get hiking!

Segment 1 begins at the Waterton Canyon Trailhead along the South Platte River, west of Denver. This canyon is popular with day-hikers, mountain bike riders, runners, and fishermen, so we had company on the first seven miles as the Colorado Trail shares a gravel service road that accesses the impressive Strontia Springs Dam. From here the trail leaves the road, and the crowds, and ascends steeply as the route gets more difficult.

The trail from this point on got pretty dicey. The warmer early-spring days would melt the snow under the pines, and the water would stream down parts of the trail, but then freeze with the still cold nights. The whole cycle would start again the next day; so many parts of the trail were sheeted with thick ice. Great, an ice rink on a mountain trail. It was nearly impossible for us to traverse uphill. It requiring us to straddle the muddy edges, or negotiate an alternate route through a part of the woods around the accident-waiting-to-happen. We didn't even consider standing on the descents, but instead slid wildly out of control on our rear ends. Even with careful attention, we slipped and fell many times.

We stopped several times to rest. Who knew falling down so much would be so exhausting? We were beginning to rethink this whole nearly 500-mile hiking thing. Our trail snacks of raisins, peanuts, and M&M's made us feel better. Cake would have helped. And a large thermos of hot chocolate.

The almost 17-mile trail should have taken us about nine hours to complete, but, at this slowed pace, we were *way* off schedule. With the sunlight waning, we were still miles from the car. The temperature was dropping and would reach a low of 13 degrees. We were spent, but if we didn't keep moving, we'd become trail-sicles!

We could hardly see the car in the moonless dark at the parking area at the end of this first trail section. Diane shuffled over to the SUV and hugged and kissed it. I was afraid her lips would stick to the hood.

One CT segment down—27 to go. Just another 451 miles. For future trail sections, we would need to temper our passion with good planning. Given what distance we had set out to accomplish, we did need to *live* long enough to complete it!

The End

We had hiked a truly unbelievable amount of miles together on the Colorado Trail. A goal that seemed nearly unachievable when we started. It was quite a commitment, and took several years because we chose to do it in sections, rather than as a through hike.

Here we were on a mountain path on our way down to Durango, the last CT segment—trail's end! All the way from Denver. All those miles, all those challenges, all those stories behind us. Had we really accomplished this? Our feet would testify that we'd done it!

I had always warned Diane for the long segments not to ignore her body's attempt to get her attention, and the earlier, the better. Some aches and pains on a lengthy hike are to be expected, but issues like "hot spots" on your feet should not be neglected to the point where they become nasty blisters.

My dear wife is either stubborn, has a very high tolerance for pain, doesn't like to stop (even for trail snacking), or all of the above. I'm going with all of the above. Such was the case on Segment 28—Kennebec Trailhead down to Junction Creek—our "final lap." About halfway through this 21.5-mile endurance test, she happened to casually mention—without complaining, mind you—some minor discomfort with her feet. I suggested we take a look, But, no, she was determined to keep moving.

Tales from the Trails

This stunning segment in the San Juan Forest (one of our favorite regions of the CT) passes through dense forests, through a narrow canyon and trends downward, losing 4,700 feet. It offers relative downhill ease (except to have to "put on the brakes" a lot), but does not shorten the distance we had to travel.

At about mile 15, Diane was hobbling. At mile 20, she was crawling on all fours. I had to drag her the last 100 yards to the finish line. (I exaggerate, but just a bit.) Seriously, when we reached the car, she really could not walk. Upon examination, we discovered she had two monster blood blisters the size of breakfast bagels on the bottom of each foot. I had never see anything like it.

We had rooms at the Pagosa Springs Resort and had planned to reward ourselves for a job well done with a good soak in the hot springs. This was also a celebration for completing the very last segment of the Colorado Trail. The only way to get Diane down to the soothing pools from our room was to carry her "horse-y" style through the parking lot. Her poor dogs didn't heal for weeks.

I know that on long trail hikes, one has to pay attention to the little things and take care of them before they become big problems. I think Diane knows that now. We'll see.

Such is life off the mountain too. We can't ignore the warning signs that trouble may be brewing. Just ask Diane's feet.

The Playful Hand of God, and Joe

Joshua Tree National Park, Mojave Desert, California

*Three guys were walking in a desert.
Each had an item he had brought with him for the trek.
The first said, "I have this watermelon to quench our thirst."
"I brought this umbrella to shade us from the sun" said the second guy.
The third guy dragged a heavy object behind him. "I brung this car door so when we get hot we can roll down the window."*

Dumb joke. Sorry. Like one my loveable son-in-law, Joe Thompson, would tell. Now, in his defense, with his fun personality, he is the nearly constant playmate for our granddaughter after dinner. We're not sure whose silliness rubs off on whom.

My wife, our daughter, Sarah, her husband, Joe, and I, all spent a long day in Joshua Tree National Park on our way to business in Southern California. We would need a car for the week in Pasadena, so we drove from our home in Colorado. I wasn't going to miss a chance to take a side trip to visit this natural marvel in the Mojave Desert. We started out early for our desert day, brought plenty of water (no watermelons), and left the doors on the car.

The half million acres of the park represent one of the most unusual locales you would ever visit. It's almost as if after the seventh day, God rested and played in this vast sandbox, stacking giant boulders into tower piles. The already surreal moonscape is scattered with these monolithic heaps impossibly placed in the middle of nowhere. But this is only the start of the wonders of the place. And Joe would help us to discover other whimsy found in this otherworldly setting.

Tales from the Trails

The desert here is immense and varied, having been shaped by rare, sudden torrents of rain and extreme climatic changes. Seasonally, it's ridiculously hot, arid, empty, yet full of life. Dotting the scenery throughout the park like abstract exclamation points is its namesake, the Joshua tree.

When they observed the branches of this odd member of the Yucca family, early settlers—understandably few, as most just looked around and then continued on to Laguna Beach—were reminded of the Old Testament prophet Joshua waving the children of Israel into the Promised Land. They look like something post-apocalyptic to me, from the book of Revelation.

To call this tree picturesque, as some do, is kind. To be fair, this is a harsh environment. Tough on the complexion and hairdo. And, the Joshua Trees are old, really old. I guess I'd hope to look even half this good at their age. The tallest tree in the park stands 40 feet high, and at a growth rate of one-half inch per year, experts estimate this old fella is more than 900-years old.

Compared to the mighty oak, the giant sequoia, the majestic blue spruce or brilliantly colored red maples, this poor tree must really have an inferiority complex. But, then, it hasn't traveled much, found only in the southwestern United States. It does have the distinction of being used for the title of a 1987 U2 rock album. How many scraggly trees have that claim to fame?

Since we had little time to visit, we drove through the entire park, and selected just two of the 111 well-described hiking trials to explore. Our first stop was the popular Barker Dam Loop. We were early enough in the season possibly to have the rare chance see water in the man-made desert reservoir, and the picture-perfect reflection of the boulders that ringed it.

When hiking with Joe, we came to discover, you have to keep your eye on him, like a small child. At that time, he was an engineer for an electric car company—one of the brightest guys I know. Wicked smart. But his mind seems to be constantly looking for mischief. So we are on him to behave, at least in public, to stay out of trouble and to not hurt himself. As his parents (in-laws), we don't want to see him taken away from our daughter, or us, and sent to jail, the hospital, or foster care. At the very start of the trail, not 10 yards from the parking area, we had to ask him not to chase the friendly jackrabbit.

We were not disappointed by Barker Dam, built in the late 1800s by cattlemen. Arriving in March, we had not only beaten the heat, but the spring runoff had filled the lake to near capacity. To see this in the middle of the desert was amazing!

Of course, Joe saw this as an opportunity for adventure and (harmless) misbehavior. He was convinced that pushing our screaming daughter—boulder-hopping smooth, half-submersed rocks—out into the middle of the water would make for a better photo op. It did, but I'm sure he had a few bruises on his arm from the punching.

On the shore, it was Joe, naturally, who discovered "Butt Rock," a large boulder that was shaped, well, like a plump posterior mooning the landscape. Of course, we all had to take a turn for the camera, posing, bent over, next to the uncannily, anatomically correct natural sculpture. Note for the little ones: we did all keep our pants up around our waist, the rock only going au natural.

We left the reservoir, having to ask Joe to stay off the narrow top of the dam, and we dropped lower to a large open park. Surrounding us were boulder piles as tall as buildings, scrubby plants shouting for water and the iconic Joshua Trees. In the distance, snow-capped peaks created a dramatic backdrop to the already jaw-dropping landscape. Sarah, a professional portrait photographer, had loads of fun stretching her wings on scenic shots.

"Hey, look at this!" we heard, as we sauntered down a sandy trail.

We turned to see Joe holding a six-foot log over his head. Now, he did train as a wrestler for the Olympics at one time, and we knew he was strong, but this was ridiculous. He pumped the dead tree over his head like it was made of paper mache. Either that or he was far more robust than we had previously imagined. He danced around and twirled the log like a huge baton. We discovered that a Joshua Tree, when dead at least, dried out of all its substance, was as light as balsa wood.

A short offshoot trail took us to a rock nook with vivid Native American petroglyphs too brightly colored to seem authentic. Turns out they were real, but the drawings had been enhanced by a location director for an old Hollywood western to make them look crisper. Nothing like improving on the originals.

Joe decided he needed a better look, up close. He climbed up into the alcove. We all shouted that we didn't think that was a very good idea, inappropriate, if not illegal, and that he should get down, now. Just a second, he requested.

It was at this precise moment that a park ranger and about 50 school children on an educational desert trail hike came around the corner. Embarrassed—in fact we were all red-faced mortified for letting our adult-youngster get out of our reach—Joe eased down the rock face and shambled back to the main trail, ears pinned back, and tail between his legs. I didn't know if park security would be called, or child protective services.

The desert wilderness is a place for exploration and discovery. There is freedom here, a refuge for the human spirit. A place for learning, and for play. And, if approached responsibly, a place for a whole lot of Joe-style fun!

Mistakes Happen

Crestone Peak, Crestone Needle, Humboldt Peak, Sangre de Cristo Mountains, CO

"Good judgment comes from bad experience,
and a lot of that comes from bad judgment."

— Author unknown —

Someone once asked, "How come dumb stuff seems so smart while you are doing it?" My adult son, Cary, and I hadn't started out this September morning to create such challenging conditions for ourselves, nor concern our loved ones so much. Our plan made sense at the time. If we could check off at least two 14,000 ft. peaks, and possibly three, from our climbing list, we wouldn't have to drive up a horrible 4-wheel-drive road (one of Colorado's roughest) a second time. Brilliant.

Most climbers approach these three Peaks—the two Crestones (connected by a dramatic sawtooth ridge) and Humboldt Peak—as three separate excursions. That's what we *should* have done. If "experience is the name everyone gives to their mistakes," then we gained lots of experience on this trip!

We hadn't planned to summit Humboldt Peak (elevation 14,064 ft.) this same outing, but it was "on the way" to the Crestones, in the neighborhood, and we really did not want to drive up that ridiculously rough 4x4 road another time. To say that this is a road at all is a stretch. Like most Jeep trails in the Sangre de Cristo Mountains, this one was steep, loose, and covered with either boulders or "baby head" rocks just screaming to wreak havoc to your vehicle. Kevin did about $1,500 worth of damage to his SUV on his crawl up. It took us about an hour and a half to negotiate the 5.2 miles to the South Colony Lake Trailhead.

The morning was cloud-free and gorgeous, and the day stayed that way. To get to the base of the Crestones, we had to hike past the South Colony Lakes and then the trail ascended to Humboldt Saddle. Along the way, we were treated to the close sight of a large herd of Rocky Mountain Bighorn Sheep, grazing on bright green meadows peppered by jagged rocks. They looked up, chortling at the fools who passed.

This route required us to climb to the saddle below Humboldt Peak. We didn't want to drive that wicked road again, so it was at this point that we decided to add another 14er summit to our day. This was a mistake, as we added about a mile round trip hiking, exerted extra effort, and ate up precious time. We assumed that the quick side trip would not impact our overall plans much. We assumed that the Crestones would not be as difficult to climb as the books stated. We forgot Wethern's Law: "Assumption is the mother of all screw-ups."

Having conquered our Humboldt detour, we worked our way across Bear's Playground, looking around warily, wondering if this area was aptly named. We then traversed a ledge system above cliff bands to the North Couloir that leads to the top of Crestone Peak. This steep gully greeted us with loose rock and dirt—not a climb we'd want to do with any other climbers above us, but this day, we were all by ourselves. Our ascent was slow and difficult, real hand and foot stuff (I try not to use the word "dangerous" when reporting our climbs back to my wife) but we finally summited our second peak around 4:30 pm.

Understand that the goal in climbing any 14er is to be up and off the top by noon, to avoid afternoon thunderstorms. We were a bit off schedule, to say the least (especially with one more peak to go), but the good weather held. Due to our less-than-optimum start time, the creep up the 4x4 trail, our side trip to Humboldt, and the challenge of the North Couloir on Crestone Peak, we were just now sitting down on top to have our lunch (dinner?) break.

T. Duren Jones

Mistake Number 2, or 3, or 4 (I'm going to stop counting) was setting down the map we were studying while we snacked. A gust of wind lifted our route directions off a rock, and in a microsecond (although, it seemed like slow motion to me) mailed it over the summit's cliff edge. Cary and I watched helplessly as it fluttered and spun hundreds of feet, then out of sight. We sat stunned; neither of us spoke.

The Crestone Peak to Crestone Needle traverse—one of the four classic traverses in Colorado mountaineering—is a challenging and complicated route, requiring experienced skills and a detailed map. We looked over the edge again, into the void. Fortunately (and I am teased about my over preparation), I had a back-up map, but it was not as detailed. Our route finding would be tested to the max.

We determined the connecting traverse was a couple hundred feet below the jagged ridge crest, and it looked very formidable from a distance. The two peaks are separated by a straight-line distance of about a half a mile, but the terrain was an intricate mess to navigate. Going was slow as we were very deliberate about not making errors. There were very few cairns to allow us to "connect the dots," and the ledges were narrow with sharp drop-offs. After a couple of hours, route finding became even more demanding and real climbing began again.

We were now close to the base of the towers called the Three Gendarmes, and could see the small Needle summit. We knew that one of the many gully or couloir choices was our route to the top. The problem was we didn't know which one, and our *simple* map didn't show us the right way up. I was pretty exhausted by now—we both were—but Cary, being the younger, more reckless, tested a couple of routes, only hitting cliff dead ends. He didn't tell me until years later that he slipped on gravel and almost fell 1,000 feet off a ledge.

I felt I had to make the call. We had really wanted to summit all three peaks this day, and were so close—within a few hundred feet. But I had told my wife we'd be careful, and that I would bring us both home safely. So far, so good, on that promise. It was 7:30 by now, and in the dimming light, we weighed our options. We would have to come back another day to bag Crestone Needle.

"Son, we just *have* to get off this part of the mountain before dark," I said with disappointment. "We've maybe got an hour of light left, and I can't imagine climbing down some of the challenging parts in the dark." He agreed, with resignation.

There was no way we were going back the way we'd come, especially thinking about descending the steep North Couloir at night. We studied our map and decided to go down to the valley below us, to Cottonwood Creek, and then climb up and over Broken Hand Pass. From there, we'd drop down back to South Colony Lakes and pick up the trail to the car. It was an ambitious plan, but we needed to get off the mountain. One series of mistakes just led to others. I regretted the situation I had allowed ourselves to be in, and wondered if I could get us down. I breathed out a sigh of a prayer and sent it heavenward.

As the light faded, we carefully inched our way down gullies, making our own trail past large rock outcroppings to the valley below. In the transition to a moonless night, the towering formations around us took on an eerie presence. We were using our flashlights well before we reached the Cottonwood Creek basin.

We stopped several times to catch our breath and drink and eat something for fuel and hydration. Most of our supplies were gone by now. We were spent.

Leaving the valley, we stopped half way up Broken Hand Pass. I turned my flashlight off to save batteries while we rested, setting it down next to me. Maybe through sheer exhaustion, possibly bordering on delirium, when we got up to continue, I walked away from my flashlight. I was following Cary, and by the time I discovered my mistake, it was too late to go back. Plodding on, we had to share one flashlight.

It was as dark as a bear's cave, so when we came to a particularly difficult section to climb down, one person would shine the flashlight for the other, and then toss the light to the one below to illuminate the rocks for the other! This technique worked ... that is, until the light became fainter and fainter as the batteries died.

We had to strike a match to have enough light to change the batteries on the flashlight. The covering over the safety matches, to protect them from moisture, makes them almost impossible to ignite. After several fumbling, failed attempts, we were back in business again. In an effort to make continued improvements to my pack, I now carry two small flashlights, extra batteries, *and* a headlamp ... and a Butane lighter.

I've come out of the forest several times in the dark, following a long hike or climb. But I'd never come down *off the top* of a mountain in ink black conditions. This was crazy. And slow. And physically and mentally grueling. At 1:30 am, we decided to call it quits.

I had a general idea where we were, based on the landmarks we'd passed and our directional progress. And this placed us, I believed, at a spot where there were cliffs below us and to our right. I had read about a hiker who had died falling over these cliffs, in a similar situation to ours. I didn't want to take any chances getting too close to what I couldn't see coming, so we stopped. We couldn't have taken another step anyway.

We collapsed where we stood. Cary exhibited several classic signs of dehydration. Having not planned for this big of a day, we had gone through all our water. Dealing with the complications of drinking water tainted with *Giardia* parasites (survivable, but miserable) beats death by dehydration. So, for the first time since I was a kid hiking in the San Gabriel Mountains in Southern California, drinking water straight from a stream, I walked to a small creek not far from us and filled our water bottles. We gulped down the most thirst-quenching drink of water we'd ever had. Then we split our last candy bar.

The night turned quite cold, which is expected for this time of year in the Rockies, especially at this elevation. We were still *way* above the tree line. We unpacked our gear and put on every bit of clothing we had as well as our rain parkas to try to hold in heat. Then we wrapped ourselves in our emergency survival blankets. Because we were still high up the mountain, there was little smooth ground to lie down on—and no leaves, pine needles, or meadow grass to provide comfort or insulation. We did the best we could.

By the way, don't let anyone tell you those emergency blankets actually work. They were useless. We lay there shivering, chilled to the bone, wrapped in a marketing concept. The idea is that it's designed to reflect your body's heat back at you. As far as we could see, they just provided an attention getting, shiny, aluminum foil covered, lukewarm, tasty human burrito for some wilderness predator.

Thankfully, nothing came by looking for a delivered meal of German-Irish food. During the portion of the sleepless night that remained, we did hear a pack of coyotes howling somewhere. We were sure they were wolves, or maybe werewolves, which, of course, was totally irrational due to the moonless night. We tossed and turned on our bed of rocks for the next few hours until dawn. All I could think about was: how could I have done this? And how much must this have worried my poor wife? I knew Cary and I would be okay—we were experiences hikers, and came *somewhat* well prepared. But Diane would only imagine the worst had happened to us.

With the warming sunrise transforming the landscape from gray to yellow-orange, we could see we were safely between the two cliff drop-offs. And, from our vantage point, we could see we were only a few hundred yards from the trail back to our SUV. We shook off the cool morning and stiff muscles, loaded on our packs, and headed to the path home.

It was a very strange experience to have two hikers holler up the trail to us, "Hey, are you guys Tim and Cary?" The Custer County Search and Rescue had been called by Kevin, at the request of Diane. Kevin had known where we were going and what our basic plans were. We sheepishly greeted the volunteers, embarrassed by our blunder, and sorry they had to come and find us. They were glad we were safe.

We were so curious, had they continued their upward trek, how they would have known where to find us. They said they had spoken to Kevin, and knew what we intended to accomplish—they also surmised that if plans didn't go as expected, we'd devise a good Plan B. They narrated assumptions of our route and predicament exactly as it had occurred. We were all glad that their rescue didn't end in a body recovery. We offered to express our appreciation by buying them breakfast in Westcliffe. They said they could not accept that, but could bring back a donation to the county Search and Rescue, which we gratefully gave. I called Diane as soon as we got down to the valley.

We learned some **dos** and **don'ts** of alpine climbing from this trip—our attempt at a 14er triple-bagger day:

- ❖ ***Do*** know your capabilities;
- ❖ ***Don't*** bite off more than you can chew. Like trying to summit three peaks in one day, especially if two—Crestone Peak and Needle (elevation 14,294 ft., 14,197 ft., respectively)—are extremely difficult ones to climb
- ❖ ***Do*** carry a good, detailed route map;
- ❖ ***Don't*** let it be blown off the top of a peak by a surprise gust of wind.
- ❖ ***Do*** have dreams, goals and ambitions;
- ❖ ***Don't*** be over-confident—and know when to quit (don't keep trying to find a 3rd peak's route at 7:30 at night).
- ❖ ***Do*** come prepared (have a flashlight for your hike out in the dark);
- ❖ ***Don't*** leave it behind at your last rest stop, no matter how exhausted you are.

Tales from the Trails

- ❖ ***Do*** have a well-stocked backpack;
- ❖ ***Don't*** think that two climbers sharing a Snickers candy bar, and sipping the last drops of water from your bottle (having polished everything else off from the long day) is proper fuel and hydration. Also, realize that climbing into paper-thin emergency blankets does not count as an effective bivouac for the night.
- ❖ ***Do*** let someone know where you are going, and what your expected return time is;
- ❖ ***Don't*** be surprised the next morning, if you didn't return home, to see a Search and Rescue team, called in panic by your spouse who had spent a sleepless night worrying, coming up the mountain from the trailhead.

If, as it is said, "mistakes are sometimes the best memories," then we made great memories! And, if it is true that, "it's amazing how much more you can learn by making mistakes than you can by making perfect decisions," then we learned a lot from this outing.

What started out as a challenging day in the high country became a comedy of errors, with misjudgments, which caused Cary and me to spend the night on the side of a mountain. We avoided tragedy, but in retrospect, we experienced a grand adventure that we still talk about.

We made judgment errors that day, and mistakes in the Colorado Rockies can be fatal. We adapted, however, changed our plans, made course corrections and found our way out. I am a bit surprised that my wife ever let us climb again.

We did.

Tim and Cary summit successfully on a re-do of Crestone Needle—Crestone Peak in background.

The Upside Down Mountain

South Rim, Grand Canyon, South Kaibab Trail to Bright Angel Trail

"The wonders of the Grand Canyon cannot be adequately represented in symbols of speech, nor speech itself. The resources of the graphic art are taxed beyond their powers in attempting to portray its features. Language and illustration combined must fail."

— John Wesley Powell (1834 – 1902) —

"WARNING! Danger!" read the sign at the start of the South Kaibab Trail. It continued in four languages: "DO NOT attempt to hike from the canyon rim to the river and back in one day. Each year hikers suffer serious illness or death from exhaustion." The stern caution was accompanied by an illustration at the edge of the canyon of a fatigued hiker—in 1980's white short-shorts, T-shirt, tennis shoes, with no pack or water bottle—holding his hand up to his hatless head, clearly in pain and/or disillusionment.

The National Park Service web site reports that over 250 people are rescued from the canyon each year. The information goes on to state, "The difference between a great adventure in the Grand Canyon and a trip to the hospital (or worse) is up to YOU." Naturally, Kevin and I had to do this challenge, down and up, as a day hike.

The afternoon before our great adventure, or trip to the hospital, or morgue, Kevin and I took a reconnaissance trip from our hotel in Grand Canyon Village to our trailhead. We'd be starting the next day before dawn, and we wanted to know our way around. As we looked down into the long dark canyon shadows of early evening, we considered just going to the Grand

Tales from the Trails

Canyon movie showing at the IMAX Theater in town (just a short distance from the actual canyon!) which would have saved us a whole lot of time and effort. After a dinner of my first rattlesnake meal at a cowboy café, I spent a restless night in anticipation of the ordeal to come.

The word Kaibab for our South Kaibab Trail and the Kaibab Forest bordering the North and South canyon rims is derived from the Paiute word meaning "mountain lying down," or "upside down mountain." When we peered down into the Grand Canyon with little morning light, we could understand why. I'm used to climbing *up* mountains, then back *down*. This was a challenge in reverse. We were so far away from Phantom Ranch at the bottom that we could not even see the Colorado River that had cut the canyon so deep.

As we descended in the crisp morning air, yellow-orange sunlight burst over the canyon edge. The views in every direction were breathtaking. The quote from John Wesley Powell above frees me from having to describe in any detail the beauty of this grand canyon. The great explorer of the American West was famous for the 1869, three-month, river trip down the Green and Colorado Rivers that included the first known passage through the Grand Canyon. Powell eventually became the director of the Bureau of Ethnology at the Smithsonian Institution, where he supported linguistic and sociological research and publications.

If Powell had trouble describing such a spectacular natural wonder, how could I begin to do it justice in written word? You've seen the coffee table book photographs, right? Okay, it's even more beautiful and varied in person. And it is one REALLY BIG canyon! There, description complete.

Our plan was to day hike the 6.3-mile, 4,740 ft. South Kaibab descent to the Colorado River and Phantom Ranch, and then (after a short rest) climb up the more popular Bright Angel Trail, with a 9.5-mile, 4,360 ft. ascent. A bold agenda, but it didn't appear more difficult than our seemingly equivalent Colorado Fourteener mountain climbs. Just in reverse.

Kevin holding hat in high wind at start of Kaibab Trail descent, Grand Canyon.

With jaw dropped appropriately and camera clicking around every steep switchback turn, I did well the first section on the gravely trail, catching myself from serious slips with my hiking stick. My knees held up and my toes didn't get driven too far into the front of my hiking boots.

Then, past Ooo Ahh Point (yes, lots of ooos and ahhhs) and across Cedar Ridge, at not much more than a couple of miles (into the 16-mile hike!), I started to encounter a serious problem. As I began to traverse the slopes below O'Neill Butte, I was hit with a bad case of shin splints—my guess, since I had never had shin splints before. My conclusion was that this was brought on by the steepness of the trail and the uneven, oddly distanced "steps" for the particularly difficult parts.

Shin splints (as I found out later—WebMD was not available to me in the canyon), medically known as medial tibial stress syndrome, is a painful inflammatory condition brought on by strenuous, excessive pressure activity (and in my case, downhill, probably mixed with the jerky motion needed to avoid the mule piles and puddles from the pack trains). Usually, there is injury to the bone and/or the surrounding tissue.

This brought me to a literally painful standstill, and some problematic decision-making. The only pain I've experienced close to this was when I spiral fractured my fibula, accidentally stepping into a hole on a mountain trail near my home in Colorado.

I made the bone-headed decision this time to press on, thinking I could "push through the pain" and maybe it would work itself out. What it needed was ice and rest. I probably worsened the injury and pain by continuing.

I hobbled on to Skeleton Point, clearly marked with a trail sign (but no explanation), with no skeletons visible. I was afraid that if I didn't keep moving, the sight of my vulture-picked, bleached bones on the trail might be jarring to some hikers. But the Park Service is pretty good about cleaning up the carcasses of downed guests.

My pace had slowed considerably. Every step felt like I was extending a fracture, and even doing some nerve damage. Kevin was a good distance ahead of me, out of view, recording some space epic battle scene for a new book, and completely oblivious to my dilemma. By the time I crossed the desolate Tonto Plateau, descended into Granite Gorge, took more photos at Panorama Point, and crossed the Colorado River on the Black Bridge, I was tempted to soak my aching leg in the cool water at the sandy Boat Beach. I didn't want to risk a chance of taking my boot off, and never getting it back on again. And I just wanted to cover the half-mile River Trail to Phantom Ranch and sit and rest for a while.

Phantom Ranch is an unexpected bright green oasis of cottonwood trees, scrub brush and grassy respites made possible by a nearby creek. With proper planning, and reservations made two years advance, one can spend the night (or days of quiet relaxation) in quaint cabins or picturesque campsites. I stumbled my way to the Phantom Ranch Canteen where I met back up with Kevin. We compared trail notes, and I shared, but underplayed, my injury.

American playwright, screenwriter and novelist Paul Rudnik was quoted as saying, "I believe in a benevolent God not because He created the Grand Canyon or Michelangelo, but because He gave us snacks." I hadn't had a Tecate Beer since college. That can of Mexican brew plus a snack of pretzels and Snickers was the best reward and refreshment I could have imagined! I would have liked to rest longer in the breeze under a shade tree, but we still had more than half the mileage ahead of us, and all uphill.

I took another round of Advil and we started out along the continuing River Trail a mile and a half to the Silver Bridge to cross back over the Colorado again. Much of this portion of the trail was very sandy, reminding me of the Southern California beach sand I walked across as a kid.

Remarkably, perhaps understandably, on the ascent up the Bright Angel Trail, my shin actually felt a bit better than on the downhill trail. I was still favoring the right leg, and doing a little hobble-step, but I wasn't experiencing the severe shooting pain as before. Uphill felt better—especially since the Bright Angel is not as steep as the South Kaibab Trail.

And my spirits were lifted by surprises. For all practical purposes, the Grand Canyon is a desert. But on my ascent I saw much evidence of brimming life: small streams and waterfalls, birds, squirrels, rabbits, and deer. I needed these nice *distractions* to help me keep my mind away from the pain, focusing on the goal, one step at a time.

Kevin and I are used to long hikes, even in extreme conditions, but this one was testing us to our limits. We were hot and exposed on this trail, especially at this lower elevation and at this time of day. I thought I had enough water with the refill at Phantom Ranch, but I was going through it faster than expected on this uphill section. Whether due to heat prostration, sheer exhaustion, symptoms related to the shin splints, dehydration (perhaps from the dehydrating effects of the alcohol in the beer), the rattlesnake meat from the night before, or all of the above, I began feeling lousy. Really bad. Weak and nauseated. Didn't we see a warning sign about this somewhere?

It's at times like this that idiot hikers like me simply have to call on a little *extra*. What choice was there really? I had to get back. I didn't bring the proper equipment to bivouac for the night somewhere off trail, especially since the temperature in the canyon can get quite cool at night in the springtime. And I was motivated by the fact that a good rewarding dinner, a hotel hot tub and a comfy bed awaited me at the top! So ... one more step at a time ... and one more.

This hike continued to surprise and amaze! We reached Indian Gardens to find another cool, shaded oasis covered with cottonwood trees and other vegetation. The campground and rest stop had a small creek running through it and a natural spring to refill fresh drinking water. Benches and picnic tables dotted the park-like setting for weary, thirsty, shin-splinted travelers. Late afternoon light dappled the grounds through the gently-moving leaves, and red cliffs framed the surrounding landscape. Maybe I actually died somewhere on the trail and this was heaven!

Refreshed, and as much as I was enjoying this spot, I got up and started moving again. We wanted to be out of the canyon before dark, and we still had about 4.5 miles to the top! Really? I've taken whole hikes that by themselves were less than 4.5 miles long! I stepped aside on the trail as a mule train loaded with tourists passed me. I almost put my thumb out to hitchhike a ride.

As we climbed up, up up, it was as if the trail was saying, "I told you so," echoing all the other warnings we were given. The steepest part of the Bright Angel Trail was saved for last. Those lovey red cliffs at a distance now seemed quite intimidating and had to be scaled with an endless number of switchbacks. We eventually passed Three Mile Resthouse, and then One and a Half Mile Resthouse. So close! We looked back and saw a butte called "The Battleship." Somewhere, *way* down the canyon, out of sight, was the river we had come from. Hard to believe that we had come so far, and were now so close to finishing.

I suppose it would be a more theatrical finish to this tale if, in the last 100 yards or so, I had collapsed, unable to complete the ordeal, or that Kevin dragged me the last few feet to the top, and then I had to be air-lifted to a hospital. But my bum leg and I did make it to the top, without much more drama, and to no cheering fanfare.

We had conquered the Upside Down Mountain. What an experience. It wasn't easy, to be sure, and I wouldn't recommend that someone follow our plan. I was sick for the next 3 days. My shin splints healed up in a few weeks. With all my subsequent hiking, I haven't experienced anything like that since.

John Wesley Powell struggled for words to capture the splendor of this awesome canyon, this national treasure. I think he actually did sum it up fairly well when he said, "The elements that unite to make the Grand Canyon the most sublime spectacle in nature are multifarious and exceedingly diverse." I had to look up "multifarious," and, yes, Powell nailed it.

Camping with Cannibals

Colorado Trail, Segment 14, Chalk Creek Trailhead to US-50

"Things are not always what they seem; the first appearance deceives many."

— Phaedrus (Roman writer, 15 BC – 50 AD) —

It was a dark and stormy night.... Well, it wasn't quite dark yet, dusk really. And the storm clouds that had built on a far mountain range had mercifully decided against heading our way. By the time we reached the closed campground, the curtain of darkness had dropped rapidly in this canyon. We shined our flashlights down an eroded dirt entry road. Cautiously, we walked towards the compound. The only light in the vacant facility came from a dim backroom bulb in the camp office.

○ ○ ○

Choosing not to tackle the 486-mile Colorado Trail as a through-hike, the only practical way for us to knock off the 28 segments separately is to take two cars. Kevin and I (with Diane) drive to different ends of a trail segment, park our vehicles, and hike towards each other. Diane and I then meet up with Kevin at about a halfway point, share our experiences, exchange car keys, and are on our way. A car awaits us at the end. This system had worked well.

The nearly 21-mile Segment 14 from Chalk Creek to Highway 50 snakes through the southern end of the Sawatch Mountains, passing several nearby Fourteeners. Diane and I started at the northern end, Kevin from the south. The well-marked trial, plus our maps and printed directions, kept us on course.

Tales from the Trails

Whenever we can, Kevin and I connect by long-range walkie-talkies, following each other's progress, but we mainly carry these radios for emergencies. They have a 15-mile range, and are remarkably clear, if no canyon wall gets in the way—they don't work through solid rock.

Cotton-candy clouds floated by throughout the day, breaking up the sky, and dappled light on our changing terrain from forests to creek crossings to alpine meadows. A weather front seemed to gather in the distance, but, thankfully, never moved our direction.

Down the trail, a red shirt appeared intermittently between the pine tree trunks, coming toward us. It was Kevin, and when we finally met, we visited for a few minutes, sharing trail notes and snacks. We told Kevin that he might be heading into some weather. He told us we could expect quite a long series of switchbacks at the end that would take us down to the highway. We couldn't stay and chat for long, as we knew we had about the same distance to cover as we had done so far.

After a long trail day, there is no more welcome sight than your car. On more than one occasion, Diane has hugged our SUV at trail's end. Weary after eleven hours of hiking, we descended the steep hillside to US-50. We fully expected to see an early-evening sunset glint on the windows of my SUV where Kevin would have parked the car. Diane and I sometimes play a game with the goal being: who can spot the car first. No one was the winner this day. When we arrived, the small parking area—where our vehicle should have been—was empty.

Stunned, our first thought was that our car had been stolen. We looked around frantically. This was the only place Kevin could have parked it. We quickly tried Kevin on the cell phone. No reception in this valley. I tried the walkie-talkies—they did have that nice long range. Nothing. We were stranded. Eight miles of mountain road opening into rangeland separated us from the nearest town of Poncha Springs.

We were fatigued, and more than a little concerned about our situation. We could walk, hitchhike to town, or see if we could find a ranch house to get help. We opted to walk for a while along a narrow dirt strip on the side the asphalt highway to see what we might encounter. We shuffled on the gravel, barely able to lift one foot in front of the other.

Dusk gave way to nightfall. A couple of cars sped by us early on, and we hoped that they would see our flashlights, so that we would not become some road kill to be picked on by crows the next day.

In a couple of miles we encountered a darkened private campground, set far off the road. No cheerful "welcome" sign greeted us. No "Good Sam Club" smiley face beckoned us in. We started down the rutted dirt entrance road anyway. This is the point in the movie theater where the audience is wincing and yelling at the characters on the screen not to do it!

The place was desolate, at least by what little we could see in pitch blackness. Where were all the tents and RVs? It was a cool springtime in the Rockies, but folks still go camping this early in the season. Why no warm yellow-red glow from fire pits? Where were the playful barking dogs running alongside chattering children on bikes? Why no laughter and splashing at the pool that closes at 10:00, with the sign that reads: "We don't swim in your toilet.... Please don't pee in our pool!"

A dim light shown from some back room in the campground office. We dared to walk up to the timeworn wooden porch. We feared that if there was anybody here, the owners would be like the murderous, cannibal family from the movie *The Hills Have Eyes*. When we pushed the doorbell, would a giant, radiation-altered, crazy-eyed, bald-headed man, with the crooked smile, baring razor-sharp teeth, open the creaky door to greet us?

○ ○ ○

To even entertain such ridiculous a notion was not so great an anxiety-ridden flight of imagination. The state of Colorado, it turned out, had not been exempt from what had become common in the Pioneer West: "Emergency Cannibalism." A stone's throw from here—okay, well, many throws, over several miles—sits the Alfred Packer Massacre Site, a memorial to the dinner guests (or guests for dinner) of the Lake City Cannibal. The site is just five minutes south of the Lake City miniature golf course, and features a large sign with cartoon caricatures of two prospectors, mouths agape in disbelief, as (we are left to imagine) an ax is driven into their skulls.

Alfred "Alferd" Packer (1842-1907) was a wanna-be mountain guide and prospector who was accused of cannibalism during the winter of 1873-1874. He was tried for murder, and eventually sentenced to 40 years in prison after being convicted of manslaughter. Packer served in the Union Army in the Civil War, was discharged for epilepsy, and then decided to try his luck at prospecting and *serving* mankind in the West.

In November of 1873, Packer was part of a group of men who left Provo, Utah, to seek riches in Colorado gold country in the San Juan Mountains. On January 21, 1874, he met Ute Chief Ouray, known widely as "The White Man's Friend," near Montrose, Colorado. Chief Ouray strongly urged that the party postpone their expedition until spring, since they would likely encounter severe winter conditions in the mountains. Ignoring Ouray's advice, Packer and five other meals, I mean, men, started out for Gunnison.

The mountain passes were treacherous, the avalanche danger high, and, in some places, the snow was up to their shoulders. "Guide" Alfred Packer got the men hopelessly lost and they ran out of provisions. Perhaps he should have stayed with his father's cabinet making business in Indiana. In the best of conditions, using the most expedient route, their destination was a 75-mile trip. But the group had thought it was only 40 miles and carried just 10 days of supplies. Gold fever had trumped wise counsel and good sense.

They ran out of food, energy, and will on a high gravel shelf near Lake San Cristobal, just up the mountainside from what is now Lake City. Over the years, Packer gave three differing accounts of what happened next. In his last version, he claimed that he had gone out scouting from the campsite and came back to find one man dining on roasted friend. Having murdered the others, the madman charged him with a hatchet, Packer said, and he shot him through his full stomach. He then picked up the dropped hatchet and buried it in the man's head to finish him off.

The presiding judge at Packer's trial at the Hinsdale County Courthouse didn't buy the self-defense story. It was reported in one newspaper that Judge M. B. Gerry was quoted as saying (and this was more the stuff of lore and the sentiments of the time):

"Stand up yah voracious man-eatin' sonofabitch and receive yir sintince. When yah came to Hinsdale County, there was siven Dimmycrats. But you, yah et five of 'em, goddam, yah. I sintince yah t' be hanged by th' neck ontil yer dead, dead, as a warnin' ag'in reducin' th' Dimmycratic populayshun of this county. Packer, you Republican cannibal, I would sintince ya ta hell, but the statutes forbid it."

Judge Gerry was actually quite literate and his court-recorded comments were decisively different than the above. In reality, what Judge Gerry told Packer was more articulate and poetic: "Close your ears to the blandishments of hope. Listen not to its fluttering promises of life. But prepare to meet the spirits of thy murdered victims. Prepare for the dread certainty of death." Gerry did sentence Packer to be hanged on May 19, 1883, "until you are dead, dead, dead, and may God have mercy upon your soul."

This curious story doesn't end there. "Packer the Hacker" used all the legal avenues available to him, avoided hanging, and two years later, won the right to a new trial, this time 30 miles away in Gunnison. The Colorado Supreme Court overturned his murder conviction on a technicality, but he was convicted of five counts of voluntary manslaughter and sentenced to eight consecutive years on each count.

In August of 1897, Packer wrote a long letter to the *Rocky Mountain News*, in which he told yet another, contradictory version of his story, maintaining his innocence. Newspaper reporters and politicians got involved and pressured the governor, who finally granted Packer's request for parole in 1901. Packer was offered a job as a sideshow freak (The Lake City

Cannibal?) with the Sells-Floto Circus, but he took a guard job for a couple of years at the *Denver Post* instead.

Packer finished his life managing two mines and dealt with stomach and liver ailments (hmmm …) until his death of a stroke in April of 1907. Neighbors said that Packer had been a kind man who enjoyed telling children stories of his exploits in the mountains (um … when Mother and Father weren't around?). It's said that he became a vegetarian.

Books, songs, plays, movies and documentaries have been made about, or inspired by, the story of Alfred Packer. The co-creators of *South Park* made a film called *Cannibal! The Musical*, loosely based on Packer's life. The University of Colorado at Boulder named their cafeteria "The Alferd G. Packer Memorial Grill" with the slogan, "Have a friend for lunch!"

○ ○ ○

A porch light came on and the door opened just as we were knocking, as if the camp office occupants had closely watched our arrival. A middle-aged couple greeted us pleasantly, if a little cautiously. They seemed possibly as nervous with us as we with them, yet they invited us in, and turned on additional lights. Neither held hatchets or giant rotisserie gear.

We explained our plight, with more than a hint of looking for advice and help. The couple apologized for the appearance of the campground, explaining they were the new owners, were re-modeling the facilities, were behind schedule on getting things ready for the season, and not yet open for business. They suggested that we use their landline office phone to call my brother-in-law and even offered to drive us somewhere if we needed it. If they were cannibals, they were trying to kill us with kindness.

Kevin answered his cell phone from our favorite pizza place in Salida. He shouted for us to speak up as classic rock blared from speakers in the background. At first he was as shocked as we were. He knew exactly where he had parked the car. We knew exactly where it *wasn't*.

Digging deeper into the mystery, we discovered that Kevin had parked the car—but neglected to tell us during our trail break together—across the highway, and about a mile down a dirt road where the CT picked up again, where he thought we had agreed. This had made perfect sense to him, and to us later. But we anticipated seeing our vehicle when we spilled out of the forest at the parking area by the highway. If there was a discussed, agreed-upon arrangement, our sheer exhaustion must have pushed it out of our mind.

None of us had compared notes and confirmed our trail's end plans. What seemed reasonable just hadn't been readdressed. Expectations were an assumption, but not verified. We'd laugh about it later, but right now, we had to get back to our SUV, and get out of these mountains.

The non-cannibal campground owners said they'd be happy to take us to where our vehicle was parked. The husband knew exactly where the CT trailhead started again. Both Diane and I couldn't fit in his old truck due to the many tools and remodeling supplies, so Diane stayed behind at the office. Neither of us was entirely comfortable with being separated, but if the owners had wanted to tie us up and dunk us in a giant boiling pot over an open fire, they had ample time.

Good planning and communication in life are essential. We can't assume others think just like we do. Or can read our thoughts. A lesson that applies all the more to wilderness hikes, where a miscommunication can lead to big problems.

I Fall Down a Lot

Longs Peak, Front Range, Colorado

*"Our greatest glory is not in never failing,
but in rising up every time we fail."*

— Ralph Waldo Emerson —

I have two confessions about my Colorado 14er mountain climbing—please don't think less of me:

1) I have felt like quitting several times when climbing some of the tougher ones—I rationalized that I could just come back another day, but, in reality, I wasn't sure I could do it at all;
2) I fall down a lot.

These falls on the mountains were not life-threatening, head-over-heals, screaming-like-a-little-school-girl plunges, but slips, crashes, tumbles or rolls ascending or descending a steep trail. Coming down hard on my rear end, palms, knees or ankles. Nothing too serious, just embarrassing. Falling at higher elevations, as one might imagine, punches the drive out of ambition.

In my defense, I'm really not a klutz. I think I'm quite nimble on my feet, actually. If I hadn't picked graphic design as a career, I might have chosen interpretive dancing.

In the wilderness, things sneak up and overtake you. A tree root, slippery pea gravel, wobbly boulders, slick rocks—all seem to work in concert to impede your progress and squelch your enthusiasm. The important thing is getting back up, right?

Dominating the northern Colorado Front Range, set among a sea of 13,000 ft. peaks in Rocky Mountain National Park, Longs

Tales from the Trails

Peak is named after Stephen Long, who explored the area in the 1820s. It's also a LONG, arduous ascent—8 miles to the top, with a 5,000 ft. elevation gain. The popular Keyhole Route spirals almost completely around the mountain and passes next to treacherous cliffs. A sudden summer storm can turn the Homestretch section into a snow covered toboggan run. Many hikers have died climbing this monster, on average, one per year. Yet, novice climbers from the Greater Denver Area parade up the peak each season, probably due to its proximity.

I decided, for some odd, cruel reason to take my friend and work associate, Robert West, up Longs Peak for his *first* fourteener climb. This is not the best peak to take an inexperienced climber, but then I've been accused of having poor judgment before. Robert was camping with his family near Estes Park, knew I was planning to climb Longs, apparently was looking for a scary, male-bonding experience, so he agreed to come along.

Up early, we beat some of the masses to the trailhead, but still added a mile onto our round trip from our roadside parking spot due to the swelling pre-dawn crowds. If someone's looking for a private wilderness experience, Longs is not the peak. On a summer weekend, the standard route is like walking a crowded sidewalk in New York City at lunchtime, but without all the yelling and the honking taxicabs, and the nasty smells.

After hiking four hard miles and over 3,000 vertical feet out of the forest, we made it to the Boulder Field. Once we broke the tree line we didn't have the protection of the pines. The morning winds blew through us with a fierce chill.

Robert hadn't packed enough warm clothes. Fortunately, I always have extra. From my backpack I pulled a second pair of gloves, a knit beanie and a light windbreaker—all of which Robert stiffly snuggled into with appreciation.

Now Robert was, at that time, shall we say, with a measure of kindness, a slightly larger man than I. About my age, but taller and, although fit, *fuller figured*. Plus sized. We laughed as he struggled into the zipperless windbreaker that didn't so much lay against his other clothing, as envelop him like Saran Wrap. His arms hung off to the side like propellers. That made me worry more about the wind, although I think his weight grounded him.

Crossing the vast Boulder Field, we encountered hikers returning down the trail. We thought it amazing that they had summited already and were on their way back down. How early did they have to get up? We discovered, however, that they had turned back at the Keyhole—a large, overhanging rock at 13,150 feet.

Many were retreating due to the intense winds coming up Glacier Gorge. Some were spooked by the series of narrow ledges and smooth granite slabs that had to be negotiated between the Keyhole and the long couloir called The Trough (over 1,000 vertical feet) and on to an exposed area named The Narrows. Others were turned back by altitude sickness or fatigue. One had forgotten his gloves needed to hold on to the sharp rocks. Despite the great effort folks had put in just to get to this point, many found the next sections too intimidating.

John Petit-Senn said, "True courage is like a kite; contrary wind raises it higher." Contrary winds are notorious on this area of the mountain and today was no exception. Robert was quiet. His eyes narrowed and brow furrowed as he looked up the mountain. I couldn't tell how he was processing this.

"What are you thinking?" I asked.

"Let's go up," he answered with naive over-confidence. So the big man in the little jacket and I pressed on.

Somewhere about halfway between the Trough and the Homestretch sections, I slipped and fell.

I couldn't tell you exactly how this happened. I think I slipped on some gravel on a smooth rock. Like a cartoon character that couldn't quite get traction, my feet were moving, but I wasn't going anywhere. My arms flailed at my sides, as if I thought I could take flight with the flapping.

I guess I over-compensated. All I know was, with a thud, I lay on my back about 10 feet lower than I'd been a micro-moment before. With my full backpack on, arms and legs splayed, I looked like a turtle that had been turned over on its shell.

I lay there for a few moments. Very still. Taking inventory, thinking of all the possibilities. *How bad was it? Was I bleeding? Broken bones? Head trauma?*

I didn't feel any pain. Then I remembered that shock immediately sets in with a terrible injury. *It could be serious, but I may not feel anything. Maybe I was paralyzed. Paralyzed!*

Slowly sitting up, I realized I was okay. A little embarrassed, but okay! My backpack had absorbed the full impact of the fall. All the extra supplies I carry came through for me again. I came out without even a scratch. I was blessed and grateful.

I stood, straightened my hat, adjusted my clothes, rearranged my pack straps and continued my climb. I don't think Robert had even noticed that the "more experienced" climber had gone down, and hard. If he did, he never mentioned it.

Robert and I did push on through the scrambling Class 3 category Homestretch section (some fellow climbers were actually climbing on their hands and knees), and broke through the cliffs to the summit which was flat, and the size of a football field. Even with our early start, and although many turned back at the Keyhole, amazingly, fifty or sixty climbers celebrated on the top. One elated group even popped the cork on a Champagne bottle and toasted with plastic cups. "Elevation celebration," it's called. High-fives and back pats, and hugs all around for a job well done.

Back at Robert's family campground, we shared stories of our adventure on the mountain. Even about my tumble. Robert had done very well; despite his kids telling him beforehand they were certain the big fella would never make it. How's that for a confidence builder?

Having had such a successful time, I asked Robert if he wanted to climb another fourteener; if he was ready for his next one. He politely said no. He had climbed a fourteener, and one was enough, thank you. I'm sure my fall had nothing to do with his decision. I did rise back up again, after all.

Carpe Diem, but Before Nightfall

Chesler Park Loop, Needles District, Canyonlands, Utah

"Of all the animals, the boy is the most unmanageable."

— Plato (Greek philosopher, 428 BC – 348 BC) —

Kevin had brought my young teen son, Spencer, and me to one of the most beautiful hikes we'd ever been on. Kevin is a great tour guide to spectacular trails he has been to before. Spencer and I hadn't planned to lag behind so often. What did Uncle Kevin expect? Some have described this place as the best desert day hike in America. Now, I haven't trekked all of the day hike offerings in America, but I'm going to agree anyway.

Kevin normally keeps a brisk pace on hikes, but this day, he also wanted us to cover the 11-mile loop trail in a sensible fashion to get back to the car before dark. He knew how many hours it was going to take. He had an agenda, but, clearly, he'd never taken a hike with Spencer. Spencer dramatically redefines "taking your time."

We were in the remote Needles District of Canyonlands National Park, a fantasyland of endless rugged landscapes, accentuated by hundreds of brightly colored sandstone spires. Every rise and bend in the trail offered jaw-dropping vistas of canyons, open parks, sheer-walled cliffs and surreal pink and white rock pinnacles. It was as if the Disney Imagineers had been given the park's geological design contract. If you've visited the Walt Disney Theme Parks, this area would seem to be the real-life inspiration for the ride landscapes of Big Thunder Mountain Railroad and Splash Mountain in Frontierland.

Our long, long day had started early because, in addition to the lengthy trail mileage, we had a 90-minute drive just to get to the trailhead south of Moab. Our first stop on the way to Needles was at Newspaper Rock State Monument. This cottonwood-shaded setting is one of the finest Indian rock art symbol sites found in the United States, is easily accessible from the road, and the hundreds of carvings can be viewed up close and photographed.

The exact nature and meaning of these petroglyphs recording 2,000 years of human activity is not clearly understood, with speculations about the drawings ranging anywhere from playful Native American graffiti to an actual "newspaper" chronicling events from earlier times. I can say this, and I don't mean to sound unkind: The Freemont, Anasazi, Navajo artisans were no Da Vincis, and my impression is that this art proves that past UFO activity was centered here and not at Roswell, New Mexico.

Reaching our trailhead destination, we followed well-marked main and offshoot trails on the Chesler Park Loop. Even though this is a national park, some desert navigation is needed, using simple stuff like taking sign direction, watching for cairns (especially appreciated on the slickrock portions), and not mistaking washes for the sandy trail. And, as Spencer was inclined, not frequently leaving the path to climb comely rocks, which called out temptations like frozen sirens.

"Come on, Son," I implored, "we've got tons to see, and miles still to cover." I was hoarse from my repeated pleading.

By the time we'd climbed the ridiculously steep and rugged Elephant Hill 4-wheel-drive trail, descended the foot path into Devil's Kitchen and arrived at the edge of Chesler Park, I think Spencer had scrambled up half the boulders in the district and explored each cavernous fissure in the canyon walls. I'd assume he was just behind me, only to discover he'd yet again monkey-hopped up a semi-truck-sized rock or disappeared into a crack at the base of a sandstone skyscraper. This, combined with frequent rest breaks, drink stops, trail snack pauses and picture taking opportunities, was taxing Kevin's patience. We had a schedule to keep, after all.

In addition to his dawdling, Spencer was unusually chatty this hike. I didn't have to deal with the typical, sullen teenager grunting yes or no answers, if anything at all. We were pausing and having real conversations, about all kinds of topics! I tried to keep up with discussions about video games, computer software developments, which super hero could defeat which foe, time travel, why girls were so weird, and such other important matters of the universe.

This was not to be rushed. I realized (again!) that what Spencer will remember would not be Dad's hard work and late nights at the office, but unhurried time spent together around mutual interests. I needed to be available and take the time to allow for these special moments to unfold.

We did make it around the large, circular-shaped grassy meadows of Chesler Park, surrounded by monolithic stone castles. We squeezed our way through the quarter-mile Joint Trail narrow slot canyon and got back to the car by dusk. Thanks to Kevin's encouragement, we didn't have to spend the night in the desert. And I relearned the importance of making memories. The day had been spent trying to hurry my son along the trails, but not wanting to hurry up his life.

Capture the moment. Carpe diem. And carpe funky sandstone towers.

Chili Rellenos & Heroes Who Soared

Kit Carson Peak/Challenger Point, Sangre de Cristos, CO

"We will never forget them, nor the last time we saw them this morning as they prepared for their journey and waved goodbye and slipped the surly bonds of earth to touch the face of God."

— Ronald Reagan —

Our goal when we woke up before dawn in the small village of Crestone—about an hour's drive from our trailhead—was to climb Kit Carson Mountain (14,165 ft.) from a unique route on the western side of the Sangre de Cristo Range. My son, Cary, his friend, Andy, Kevin and I stumbled sleepy-eyed out the creaky motel door and loaded our packs into my bucket-of-bolts SUV to head to the Willow Creek Trailhead.

With as many of these Colorado fourteeners as I've climbed, you'd think I'd remember the importance of getting to bed earlier, and to watch what I have for dinner the night before. Spicy salsa and chips, two chili rellenos and extra portions of refried beans are definitely not the suggested dinner of champions before climbing these monster peaks. I felt bilious and, um, gassy, but kept it (mostly) to myself.

The climb promised to be thrilling, even if my stomach was turning summersaults. I reviewed my mental list of backpack supplies and hoped I'd brought enough TP. I wasn't going to use tree bark or pine needles.

We had planned this climb for weeks and had been looking forward to summiting Kit Carson from this route. I had no idea that my most poignant memory would be crossing over Challenger Point.

Tales from the Trails

This 11-mile round trip started with warm, buttery sunshine. Sparkling flecks of light danced on the gurgling creek next to the trail. But wet, thick fog quickly stole up the canyon after us as we ascended to Willow Lake. The creeping low cloud was moving up the mountain faster than I was, rising on the morning up-currents—no surprise there, what with the steep incline of the trail, and my ... *frequent* ... stops. The gray mist eventually overtook us, creating an eerie atmosphere.

When Cary was in his teens, I could pretty much keep up with him, even lead the way. Now in his early 20s, he would out-distance me with his pace and longer legs. I'd find him around a bend periodically, patiently waiting for me to catch up. This trip, he brought Andy with him. Andy was preparing to go into the Marines, and who knew he was also part mountain goat? Weird—the hybrid looked like a real boy. Cary had a competitive challenge now, and I was older, and had wolfed down chili rellenos the night before. I had plenty of excuses for my sluggishness.

By the time I reached some rock slabs above a tall, spectacular waterfall at the east end of a beautiful lake, it seemed the others had rested, downed a healthy portion of energy snacks, napped, watched a DVD movie and wrote their memoirs. I had very little time to catch my breath before they were ready to get moving again.

Cold, low clouds surrounded us, reducing visibility to something out of *Hound of the Baskervilles*. It would be easy to get separated and lose the trail. Serious cliffs guarded all sides of Kit Carson Mountain, and the task of finding a route on a remarkable ledge system awaited us.

First, we had to get over Challenger Point. After a mile-long steep slope and some boulder scrambling near the top, we finally summited our first peak. We knew we were standing on a special mountain. It was named in 1987 in memory of the seven astronauts who died serving mankind and fulfilling passionate dreams.

On that morning of January 28, 1986, at 11:39 EST, the Space Shuttle Challenger exploded in the sky above Cape Canaveral, 73 seconds into its flight. The astronauts' families at the air base, and millions of Americans, witnessed the space disaster live. President Ronald Reagan described the tragedy as "a national loss."

Christa McAuliffe, 37, married with two children, was to be the first schoolteacher in space—picked from among 10,000 entries in a competition. Students worldwide had expected to watch a televised broadcast of McAuliffe delivering a science lesson from space. Instead, thousands of kids watched the disintegration of the shuttle in shock and disbelief.

The cloud cover over the peak added to the drama of our somber moment as we read the memorial plaque. The summit is about ten feet wide, and at its highest point on a large boulder sits a six- by 12-inch memorial bronze plaque that reads:

**Challenger Point, 14080+'
In Memory of the Crew of Shuttle Challenger
Seven who died accepting the risk,
Expanding Mankind's horizons
January 28, 1986   Ad Astra Per Aspera**

The Latin phrase means: "To the stars through aspiration." A small group sharing common interest in mountaineering and the space program had placed the memorial here.

○ ○ ○

We pressed on to Kit Carson, dropping to a saddle between the two peaks. I completely lost the others in the dense fog, but still could negotiate my way. My lower intestinal discomforts were forgotten amidst thoughts of the Challenger crew and their families. I felt ridiculous for the under-my-breath complaining.

I did catch up with the other guys and we all then ascended to the key to this route, a large, amazing ledge system called "Kit Carson Avenue." We carefully scrambled hand over foot up a wet gully to the summit pyramid. Surprisingly, the clouds broke around us as we reached the top and we sat in warm sunshine to have a quick bite of lunch and to survey the panorama.

On the east side of Kit Carson Mountain, just a half-mile from Challenger Point, sits its companion, Columbia Point. This peak was named in memory of the seven astronauts who died when the shuttle Columbia broke up on re-entry into Earth's atmosphere February 1, 2003. At the naming of the mountain, NASA Administrator Sean O'Keefe said, "When people look upon these mountains, they see the challenge of the American frontier—bold in vision, courageous in spirit and endless in horizon."

U.S. Interior Secretary Gale Norton said future space crews would be able to look down on Earth and know the Columbia mountain peak commends the astronauts who went before them. "The point looks up to the heavens," she said, "and it allows us, once again, to thank our heroes who soared far beyond the mountain, traveled past the sky—and live on in our memories forever."

Back down in the valley, the reflections really sank in. It can all end so quickly. My life, whether long or short, is really just a moment, a breath, the blink of an eye. In the end, in the brevity of my existence, will I be able to look back and see a life well lived?

I'm fairly certain I will never have a peak named after me. No brass plaque will face heavenward telling of my accomplishments. Nor should there be. No words will read, "He survived two monster chili rellenos climbing Kit Carson Mountain."

I would hope I might simply be remembered for a life of faith and hope, of loving service to others, and whether I made a difference in anyone's life. These are the things that any one us can hope for, as we, from the mountains, courageously turn our gaze to the heavens.

Mischief in Moab

Canyonlands and Arches National Parks, Utah

"You are never too old to do goofy stuff"

— From the Television Show *Leave it to Beaver*,
Spoken by the Character Ward Cleaver —

One of my favorite places to hike is in, and around, the Moab area, in southeast Utah. This region is known for its beautiful red rock scenery, two national parks, slick rock mountain biking, 4-wheel-drive trails, canyoneering, western movie site landscapes, and Colorado River trips. Two of the people I have the most fun with are my wife, Diane, and my son-in-law, Joe. So it seemed that a trip to Moab with these two would be a perfect match. Like Diane and I, Joe also loves the outdoors, but maybe for different reasons.

I really enjoy the high desert in early spring and fall (too hot in the summer), but have also delighted in trekking through a few inches of fresh snow in the wintertime. I have been out to Moab countless times with Kevin, but also with my son, Spencer, and with other family and friends. Kevin and I have hiked all the trails that drop off the Island in the Sky mesa in Canyonlands National Park, have done quite a few other trails together around Moab, and also trekked in the amazing Needles District, about 70 miles south and west of Moab.

What I had always wanted to do was to get Diane and Joe out there to share some of my experiences. I knew Diane would love the hiking in this spectacular setting. I knew that for Joe, it would be about the *fun*. Joe can turn anything into fun.

One spring, I had the unexpected chance to take Joe and Diane to Moab (or, more accurately, be taken by Joe). Joe was asked by his employer at that time to run an experimental car part out to an engineer near Moab, stay until the part was repaired, and the company would pay for all his expenses. We all jumped at that opportunity! Diane and I could go along, help with the driving, keep Joe company (and out of trouble), and I could act as tour guide.

I love taking people out to Moab, especially first-timers, and have developed a couple of "tour packages" that I call (with tongue firmly placed in cheek) "A Taste of Moab," a two or three day introductory trip, and "The Moab Experience," a four-day, more in depth, excursion. Either of these trips can only give an overview, leaving so much more for other visits. Our time for this trip would be a compressed *taste*, but I would try to pack in as much as I could.

Our adventure had a peculiar start. Joe couldn't depart for Moab until after work. As is it about a seven-hour drive from our home (not taking into account a meal or gas stop), our arrival time would be quite late. I had fortunately researched ahead of time for a hotel reservation, only to find out that *every* room in Moab was taken for a road bike festival! We ended up having to stay in Green River, about an hour outside of Moab.

Joe had arranged a nocturnal drop off of the auto part that his electronic engineer contact was to work on. He lived about 30 miles from Moab, and had given sketchy directions to his home in Castle Valley. This was before the popularity of car GPS units or cell phone navigation and his place was probably off the grid anyway.

So here we were, driving in pitch-black darkness, in dead quiet, in the middle of the night, around an unfamiliar little desert town, looking for a house with no numbers, in a place with no street lamps, or even any posted street names. I halfway expected to see porch lights flickering on and sleepy-eyed, toothless, bearded men in pajamas and cowboy boots, holding shotguns emerging and wondering who these unwelcome, yellow-bellied varmints were.

The fact that we found the right house and dropped the part on the porch, without being shot dead in our tracks, was amazing. We'd be back in the daylight Sunday afternoon to pick up the repaired part. Exhausted, we arrived at our welcome hotel rooms at 2:00 a. m. Joe had already started our weekend off with fun!

I have said this many times: every great adventure starts with a good meal. Joe has a corollary saying that every good meal should be a BIG meal, preferably with meat. He's also said that, "everything goes better with bacon." So, naturally, our Moab adventure Day One started with breakfast at the Moab Diner.

Diane and I told Joe that he didn't really have to order one of everything on the menu, smothered in salsa, plus extra bacon. We reminded him that there were no public restrooms in the wilderness. He was undeterred. He told us that he was practicing for some upcoming power-eating competition.

Due to our time constraints, I'd only be able to get Diane and Joe an introduction to Canyonlands and Arches National Parks. For our first day, I opted to take them to Island in the Sky in Canyonlands. The Island in the Sky region is an isolated, broad, and level mesa between the Colorado and Green Rivers, with sheer sandstone 1,200 ft. drop-offs and huge wilderness landscape views.

Our first stop was Mesa Arch, via a half-mile round trip nature trail. Mesa Arch spans 50 feet across the top of a 500 ft. cliff. The arch provides a frame for a stunning Utah scenery of spectacular canyons and natural towers, with the La Sal Mountains in the background. Being so close to the main road, it has easy access and is a very popular tourist photo op. Upon arrival, few might have expected to see a breakfast-bloated silhouette on the top of the arch, backlit by the bright morning sky, striking the pose of a Greek god. The sight of Joe provided either delight or repulsion to their experience.

Our next stop was out to the southernmost point of the mesa, the Grand View Overlook. This amazing setting offers panoramic, near-endless views of a complex network of canyons cut by the Colorado and Green Rivers. A wonderful, moderate two-mile round trip trail winds its way around the cliff edge.

Tales from the Trails

At one point, Joe and I could step out on a short peninsula outcropping while Diane shuddered. As we looked straight down the 1,000 ft. drop on three sides to the shelf below, Joe had the hare-brained idea of grabbing me and beginning to stage a faux Greco Roman wrestling match on this narrow precipice. Diane shrieked for us to stop as she continued to snap pics. At least she'd have a photographic record for the park officials, and for the coroner.

Further down the trail, Joe pretended, with arms flailing, to be falling over the edge. Diane and I would have to turn our backs on him, and walk away, so as not to encourage him in that behavior. "We're not *looking*!" we shouted back.

Tim and Joe wrestle Greco-Roman style on overhang at cliff edge, Grand View Point, Island in the Sky, Canyonlands National Park.

T. Duren Jones

The end of the firm-sandstone trail took us to Grand View Point, with awesome views of Junction Butte, and, in the distance, the Needles and Maze Districts of Canyonlands National Park. Diane and I had a small trail snack as we watched Joe slide over the cliff edge to a small ledge. Despite our protestations, he wanted a photo of himself climbing back up, as if he'd just ascended the whole 1,000 vertical feet.

A bundle of energy and quite spry for his post-Olympics training weight and late 30's age, Joe then began to scramble up a large mushroom-shaped rock formation next to us. Climbing up proved to be a lot easier for him than scooting back down. We watched in amazement as he inched his way backwards on his generously proportioned stomach.

"A little help here?" he implored, as his feet dangled, not reaching a foothold.

"You got yourself up there; you can get yourself down!" I shouted. We let him hang there for a while before finally coming to his assistance and guiding his feet to firm footing. Back to the car, with his seatbelt on, with the child safety lock engaged, we could keep a good eye on him.

After a few more view points and overlooks, mixed with a couple of short hikes, we completed our limited overview of Island in the Sky. We had left a lot to see for another trip. Joe *mostly* behaved himself the balance of the day.

Our kick-start breakfast the next morning was at the popular Jailhouse Café in downtown Moab. The café actually was an old jailhouse at one time, and was the county courthouse in the late 1800's. Their fat ginger pancakes are quite tasty, and they have the best, maple-sweetest, most delicious bacon in the world. Joe had a second helping, and I thought he might stay until lunch to have a B. L. T. sandwich, with extra bacon.

After our artery-clogging, waist-expanding, pace-slowing morning feast, we headed out to Arches National Park. There was only so much we could hope to see that day, but I would try to hit the highlights, many of which would have to be simple pull-out spots for photo ops. This may not have been quite the sandbox and playground time Joe was hoping for, but we did have to pick up the repaired auto part before returning home. We would have to visit this desert wonderland another day to see more.

Arches is located just five miles north of Moab. The park contains the world's largest concentration of natural sandstone arches—over 2,000 within the park's 76,000 acres. This, along with an astounding array of geological formations like sandstone fins, huge balanced rocks, and monolithic spires, make Arches a must-see stop when in the Moab area.

We were able to catch many of the best sights: Park Avenue, The Windows District, Courthouse Towers, Petrified Sand Dunes, Fiery Furnace, and Delicate Arch view point. Diane was amazed at the exceptional beauty. All the things to climb up, go over, or squeeze through impressed Joe, big kid that he is. We nearly lost him at Sand Dune Arch, as he disappeared climbing the rock maze behind the arch.

Our last stop for the day was at Devil's Garden where one trail takes visitors to several arches including Pine Tree Arch, Wall Arch, and the phenomenal Landscape Arch, with a span of 300 feet making it one of the longest natural sandstone arches in the world. An offshoot trail took us to Tunnel Arch. We thought with all the crowds at this popular tourist destination that we might be safe from embarrassment from Joe's mischievous antics. We were wrong.

With our backs turned to him, viewing the surroundings with awe, we heard Joe clearing his throat. We turned, and there, to our shock, he sat, striking a pose on a split rail fence, grinning widely, with his shirt off, his sweaty skin gleaming in the sunshine. Let me put this as delicately and generously as I can: Over the years, Joe has nicely "filled out" his once chiseled, athletic physique. He is now at a place in life where the only time he should take his shirt off in public would be to use it as a tourniquet to stop an accident victim from bleeding to death. Otherwise, best to stay covered, and keep things a mystery. Joe got the hoped-for reaction: Diane and I doubled over with laughter, and with tears in our eyes, choked out a plea to have him clothe himself again.

Joe's mischief making on this trip certainly left us with many indelible memories—some, maybe we would like to forget! I've been back out to Moab several occasions since and have experienced times of inspiration, contemplation, and breathtaking awe. But I haven't matched that time with Diane and Joe for good 'ol goofy fun! We all need that sometimes.

Blown Away

Cameron Point, Mosquito Range, Colorado

"I find the great thing in this world is not so much where we stand, as in what direction we are moving: To reach the port of heaven, we must sail sometimes with the wind and sometimes against it, but we must sail, and not drift, nor lie at anchor."

— Marjorie Holmes —

Until just recently, I didn't know if anyone had actually been blown off a Colorado 14,000 ft. peak. I didn't think it possible. But it surely would be horrible, especially after the first 1,000 feet or so. Climbers die every year on these magnificent mountains, dispatched in any number of ways. But I wasn't aware of anyone being picked up like a kite by a ferocious wind and sent dancing in the clouds before the fatal spiral to the valley below.

Then I read of a Japanese climber who, in the summer of 2005, was blown off a ledge after reaching the summit of Longs Peak. I know how hard it is just to ascend to the summit of Longs. Apparently, for this young man, close was just not close enough for a better view from the top, and a fierce gust pushed him over the edge. He had a great opportunity, but he blew it—or it blew him (off).

It has been said, "The higher the hill, the stronger the wind." That was certainly the case as I traversed the saddle between Mt. Democrat to Cameron Point, on my way to the additional tops of Mt. Lincoln and Mt. Bross—an ambitious, but not too difficult four-peak summit in one long day. Once a certain amount of elevation was gained climbing up from Kite Lake (interestingly named), I thought I might as well try to tackle all these closely situated fourteeners by their connecting saddles.

As I summited Cameron, the wind began to pick up. Nothing stronger than I'd experienced on previous hikes. Cameron Point does climb to 14,238 feet, but does not qualify as an official fourteener because there is not enough elevation loss and gain between it and its neighbors. It only rises 157 feet from its connecting saddle with Lincoln. It must have an edifice complex. So close.

Still, as I stood on top, the mountain had a formidable feel and I remembered what the guidebook had said about avoiding the cliffs on the south face. I didn't have to be told twice—and the view from where I stood was just fine.

Curiously, as I turned slowly and surveyed the ring of these joined peaks around the cirque, the wind abruptly stopped. Nothing. Dead, and by contrast to the last hour, unsettling calm. It was almost as if the continuous wind had been sucked back into itself like a vacuum. Creepy.

I'm a prayin' man, in the city or in the wilderness, but there is just something about the great outdoors that turns one's gaze upwards. Whether sitting in a lush, emerald forest, by a clear-running stream, trekking a surreal desert landscape, or on a mountaintop with a panoramic view, when I see the beauty and wonder of nature, I'm compelled to express gratitude, and to seek something greater than myself.

This day I had brought a sailboat load of troubles from the valley up the mountain. You can imagine the emotional weight of that craft as I dragged it uphill. And how absurd and out of place it must have looked sitting on top of a 14,000 ft. peak. My own imaginary ark brought up to my personal Mt. Ararat. Now, I felt like I was stalled, anchored by the burdens of life.

Then I heard it at a distance, coming up a canyon behind me. First faint, then growing in intensity and volume. The wind sounded like a freight train charging toward my rocky peak. I turned my back bracing for the impact and planted my feet.

I had never experienced anything like this before and haven't since. The fierce wind roared up over the top as if it had taken form. It hit me in the back like a solid object and knocked me forward. But it didn't stop there. It kept pushing me toward the cliff edge.

I had to reduce my resistance and find a way to hold on. I dropped, laid down flat on my back and held tightly to rocks on each side of me. I must have looked ridiculous, but there was no one around to amuse. In what seemed like forever—just moments, I'm sure—the wind passed over me, its caboose nothing more than a trailing breeze. All was still again. I tried to reflect on what had just happened.

What was that? I do know a little something about the physics of the Laws of Thermodynamics; that the air in the valley heats with the warming of the day and rises up the mountain canyons. I'd experienced this climbing mountains many times before. But this seemed like something *way* different.

George MacDonald said, "There are other winds in the world besides those which shake the fleeces of sheep and the beards of men."

I removed my backpack and sat for a while in the tranquil wake. I munched on some trail mix and thought about troubles back home and at work. What was I afraid of? I climb 14ers, for heaven's sake—I should be able to take on anything!

Was it that I feared life's challenges back down in the valley? Did I perceive that the winds of difficulties would be too much to handle? That avoidance would be better than to confront the issues. Winston Churchill is quoted as saying, "Kites rise highest against the wind—not with it."

I felt a release that day. I sent my worries with the wind into the cobalt blue sky. Did the problems go away? No, but the burden to carry them sailed away on a cloud tide.

○ ○ ○

I did summit all four peaks that day. No wind greeted me from the top of the remaining two. I made it back to my SUV in the parking area well after dark, the only vehicle left. I still think about that day.

The wind. Friend or foe? I'm going to accept it the way a bending tree does as all the dead leaves are cleaned out in a blustery fall day. The strong branches bow low at the wind's arrival. I'm going to use it to fill my sails and to keep me moving toward a far shore. I'll receive it as a messenger, bringing hope to challenging situations.

The Marine and the Giant

Castle Peak, Elk Mountain Range, Colorado

*"Courage is being scared to death
... and saddling up anyway"*

— John Wayne —

Cedric came barreling down on me across the steep snowfield like some kind of roaring locomotive that had jumped its track ... all 6 ft., 5 in., 275 lbs. of him. I stood with my back to a huge glacial rock pile, bracing myself for his impact, in some vain effort to try to stop his out-of-control sliding descent. If I didn't halt the big man, he would fly into the sharp-edged boulders. And if I did try to save him, I was afraid, with his accelerating momentum, he'd snowplow us both over the pile and into the rocky field beyond.

○ ○ ○

I have climbed Castle Peak (14,265 ft.) three times. One time was needed toward my goal of topping all of Colorado's 14ers—the 54 mountain peaks over 14,000 feet. My first summit of Castle Peak, near Aspen, Colorado, was with Kevin. We were amazed by Castle's iconic shape and its classic trail that includes carefully crossing the steep, permanent Montezuma Glacier.

Two additional times, I took others up because of my desire to share the experience of one of my favorite mountain climbs. The views from the top are quite impressive in that the panorama includes five other fourteeners: the two Maroon Bells, Pyramid Peak, Snowmass and Capital Peak with its infamous Class 4 "knife-edge" trail section. My last trip up Castle Peak was special, as I climbed it with my granddaughter, Maren. It was her first fourteener, and we made our own stories that we will retell for a lifetime. Each unique climb provided its own memories.

The one that might hold the most poignant recollection for me was the time I climbed Castle Peak with my Marine Corp son, Daniel, just home from his first combat tour of duty in the War in Iraq. Daniel was in the 1/5 Expeditionary Unit and had been in the first wave of U. S. military forces involved in the taking of Fallujah. The Marines would have secured the city from the insurgents in a week and a half, had not the bureaucrats called our men back for political reasons. I knew what courage it took for him to be in deadly combat, but he approached his service with humility and professionalism, thanks to his training.

Daniel was on leave from the battle theater. He had accepted my invite to climb his first 14er with me, joined by my friend Bruce Peppin, his son, Brooks, and another friend, Cedric Taylor, coming for his first 14er too. Five of us packed into my Chevy Tahoe—no small feat for five men, their climbing packs, and overnight bags—and drove the four and a half hours to the posh, yet quaint, mountain town of Aspen.

We met up with another friend, Bob McCrea, and his wife, Polly, who were vacationing there. Bob would join us on our climb. We enjoyed walking together and window-shopping the fashionable downtown district, with streams running through the beautifully landscaped center strips, and baskets of lovely pansies hanging everywhere. We ate at a quirky below-street-level Mexican restaurant (maybe Mexican food wasn't the best choice before a mountain climb), and retired early.

Daniel was still wired—perhaps a combination of being safe at home with nobody shooting at him, and being excited about the climb—so he stayed out longer. He browsed the closed shops, and poked his "high-and-tight," close-cropped head into the classy restaurants and bars. As it turned out, he made several new friends that night, as many of the patrons wanted to thank him for his service to our country, buy him a beer, and hear stories from Iraq. People were curious to learn of the daily life of the military over there, of their progress in the war (nonclassified, of course), the soldiers' relationship to the general populace of peaceful Iraqi people, and typically what Middle East life was like. Daniel said he felt genuinely appreciated, and was treated like a celebrity, in this exclusive mountain community of the Hollywood Stars, of all places!

As with other 14er climbs, we were up before dawn to start our day. We drove to a narrow, winding 4-wheel-drive dirt road that would take us to our trailhead. We chugged slowly up the rugged old mine road just wide enough for our vehicle. Because there were now six of us in a SUV that barely seated five, Daniel had volunteered to sit in the back cargo area for the bumpy ride. (He said it wasn't much worse than the Humvee rides across the desert outside of Baghdad.) There were areas where the erosion was so bad or fallen boulders so numerous, that Cedric had to get out and walk ahead of the vehicle to help direct me to steer incrementally a little left or right to avoid major pitfalls, or a crushing tumble into the steep canyon below.

At the trailhead, Cedric was looking green, despite his ebony features that were in stark contrast to the snow-covered backdrop. Even at his age and with the extra weight he was carrying, he was a fit athlete, still playing basketball two to three times a week with much younger guys. But, this was his first fourteener, and his first time at this elevation. Altitude sickness is unpredictable. For some, this malady is caused by ascent to a high altitude and the corresponding shortage of oxygen, and is typically characterized by hyperventilation, nausea, headaches, and exhaustion.

Cedric said he felt a little *funky*, and we agreed it matched his appearance. But he was game to make a go of it, hoping his queasiness and headache would pass. Being his first 14er—really his first high altitude hike—we knew that this took a tremendous amount of fortitude on his part. But this was something he wanted to do, to experience with his buddies. Vincent Van Gogh is quoted as saying, "What would life be if we had no courage to attempt anything?" We'd be wise to lend an ear to listen to that advice.

We had Cedric drink plenty of water, and force down a trail snack. In a few minutes, he seemed to be feeling better. By contrast, Daniel, despite coming from desert-sea level, said he felt great, even with little sleep from the night before.

We started our steep climb by picking our way up a glacial rock pile. It was tough, finding a path around, or over, sharp-edged obstacles through this vertical boulder field. It was slow, but we had had an early start, and the sky was sunny, so we still thought we'd summit before any afternoon thunderstorms.

Cedric was really struggling. His slow pace was separating him from our little pack. I held behind to try to encourage him, literally step-by-step, as he looked skyward for help, his "Preacher's Roll" (his term) at the back of his neck accentuated by the tilt of his head. Both his father and his grandfather were ministers, and Cedric said they all have that fold from sending so many prayers heaven bound.

When we reached the base of the permanent glacier, everyone but Cedric was still doing really well, with Daniel and Brooks being exceptional, showing no signs of fatigue. Most of the group tried to find a way around the snowfield through the boulders off to the side. The young men went right up the middle, carefully finding or kicking and stomping new footholds to scale the steep ascent. One slip would take them all the way down to the bottom again, and probably in pieces.

The glacier route was tough, and negotiating the wobbly rocks at the edge may have been even more difficult, with the angle of ascent, combined with the lack of stability. About halfway up this section, Cedric began to lose his energy bar breakfast. Any benefits from his hydration and snacks went out the front door. Hands on knees, he wretched again and again. And when his hands were not on his knees, the poor guy held them to his pounding head.

The best remedy for altitude sickness is to get the ailing person back down to a lower elevation as quickly as possible. I suggested that he turn back to the car. He could rest there and wait for our return. I had already summited this peak, so I offered to go back down with him. He assured me that after he had lost his breakfast, and probably his Mexican dinner too, he actually felt a little better, and wanted to press on. This gentle giant looked heavenward again for help, and I joined him. We continued on.

At the top of the glacier, we gathered at the edge of a large cirque, the bowl creating the framework for this section of the Elk Mountains that includes Castle Peak and Conundrum Peak, closely connected by a saddle. Conundrum is not an official 14er because it doesn't meet the criterion as a separate peak, being short of the 300 ft. drop and rise requirement. We had snacks in this basin and discussed our next segment of climbing challenge. Bruce, Bob and the young climbers were ready to tackle a rugged ridge that would take us to the summit.

Clouds were building surprisingly fast, and unexpectedly at 10:00 a.m. Cedric wisely opted to stay at the bowl rim and wait for our return, but he was insistent that I summit with Daniel for the father-son memories. He said he'd rest and be okay, and that we could pick him up on our way back. I hoped he didn't mean that literally.

We continued climbing up a slope with a decent trail through loose shale to a small saddle at 13,740 feet. From the saddle, we scrambled along a rocky ridge toward the top. A dark blanket of clouds now covered us, and the wind kicked up wickedly. Here was a weather front to be closely watched. This kind of dramatic summertime weather change in the Rockies was to be anticipated—one of the reasons we get such an early start. But this threat of a morning storm was unusual.

Several hundred yards from the top, the blast hit us, just as we reached a section with dramatic cliff drop offs. It moved in so fast we didn't even have time to deliberate possible options. This wasn't just a hard rainstorm, or one mixed with hail. This was a full-on snowstorm. The temperature had dropped 30 degrees in less than half an hour. The blizzard-like conditions grew worse, and snow began to collect quickly on the talus-covered route. Bob decided to turn back, yelling through the wind that he'd rejoin Cedric should we decide to go on.

Tales from the Trails

I've been turned back from several peaks through the years due to bad weather. I'm fiercely driven, and I love this challenging activity, but I don't want to die for it. The mountain will always be here another day for me to return and conquer, I'd tell myself. Of course, on this one, as with other peaks, I felt I had the responsibility for others as well.

In freezing, white-out conditions, Bruce and I asked our boys if they wanted to turn back, or press on to make a dash for the top, seeing that we were so close. They both shouted above the roar that they wanted to summit. We pulled out everything we had in our packs, and put on layers of clothing, jackets, gloves, knit caps, and parkas. Maybe this was an unwise thing to do, especially when it put our lives at risk. The simple fact that I'm writing this account gives testimony to the fact that we made it. It could have turned out much differently....

> On the morning of August 2, 2003, John and Aaron Boyles rose from their campsite by Lake Como, at the base of Little Bear (14,043 feet), getting a much later start than they had wanted. It had been nearly midnight by the time they had hiked five miles on the rough four-wheel-drive road and set up camp the night before, so they slept in. They knew that climbers try to start early so they can get up and off the summit by noon to avoid storms on the peaks, but they thought they still had time to tackle the mountain.
>
> The North Face route John and Aaron chose covered less than two miles but it took them five hours to reach the top. It is more of a wall than a trail, with hand and foot climbing on loose rock.
>
> On the summit, they barely had time to share a favorite trail snack and set up their camera for a time-release celebration shot when they felt the air fill with static electricity. The clouds had quickly become menacing and they knew what was next: thunder and lightning. They had to get down, and fast. They packed up quickly and moved west along the exposed rock

ridge on the easiest route to the valley below. Sure enough, thunder ripped through the clouds and buckets of water hit them with a fury.

The men tried moving faster, but unsteady, wet rocks kept them at a clumsy pace. It wasn't fast enough. The sky erupted in a blinding flash near the ridge and both men hit the ground. Thunder again roared above them and echoed through the canyons. John and Aaron slowly worked their way down the rocks for the next hour as a hailstorm battered the hoods of their Gore-Tex jackets and covered the trail like snow.

The route was steep. John edged down the sloppy route unto a deep gully. Aaron followed. Unknowingly, they had missed the actual trail and had now turned down into a treacherous ravine. John yelled to his son that he thought he had found a way down. It was the last thing he said.

Aaron watched his father slip and land on the loose rock below. He thought his dad might be able to stop himself, but the rain had made the slope too slick. He saw his father vanish over the next cliff, and then the next. Boulders at the valley's edge finally stopped John's fall. In disbelief, Aaron stared down for a few moments. His 52-year-old father, and companion on most of his twenty 14er climbs, wasn't moving. He yelled his name, hoping for any sign of life. There was no answer.

○ ○ ○

Higher and higher our group of four climbed, through rougher terrain, now completely covered with a half inch of snow. Visibility was down to about an arm's length. I was worried that even if we made the summit, the route back down could be quite treacherous. We couldn't see the top, but I knew it wasn't much farther. I yelled for everyone to keep going.

When we finally crested the edge of the summit, the bitter wind hit us with explosive force. The snow stung what small portion of our faces remained exposed. We realized we had actually been shielded from the worst of the wind on the side of the mountain we had just climbed. With the severe temperature drop, mixed with these brutal gusts, the wind chill factor felt like the temperature was in the teens! Ah, Rocky Mountain summertime at 14,000 feet!

No time for chitchat—too cold to talk with lips that weren't working anyway. There was no time for a rest, trail snacks, or enjoying the views from the top (nothing to see through the storm anyway). All we had time for was high-fives, and for quickly snapping a couple of "you-were-there" photos. Our fingers were so cold it was hard to press the camera shutter. It was *past* time for us to head back down.

Descending was slow and tricky: all the rocks were covered with a slippery slush. Even the stacked stone trail markers were now buried, making route finding difficult. One slip may not have meant certain death, but could have resulted in a nasty ankle sprain, or (even worse) with a tumble. I cautioned everyone to step extra carefully.

Unbelievably, the freakish storm blew past us as rapidly as it had arrived. The claustrophobic fog blanket that had enveloped us began to give way to bright white, broken clouds speeding across a sapphire sky. Shards of wet sunlight stabbed through, and immediately started to melt the snow off the rocky trail. By the time we reached Bob and Cedric the sun was fully visible; any remaining clouds trailed the southbound storm system like a caboose.

For some ridiculous reason, we thought glissading down the snowfield on our return would be a good idea. And fun. Maybe we thought, that since we survived the snowstorm, we were somehow indestructible. The grace of God should not be taken for granted!

Glissade is a French word. Loosely translated it means, "sliding completely out of control, down a steep snowfield, screaming at the top of your lungs, heading for serious injury, or death," or something like that. Perhaps my interpretation is a bit wordy, but you get the picture. And not a pretty picture at that.

I had done glissading before. It's often a fast and enjoyable way to get down sections of 14ers. It's also a great way to really wrench one's knee, as you try to "break" momentum … like I did on Gray's Peak. Imagine speeding downhill on your rear end on a giant ice slide, with little ability to control direction and speed, and almost no way to stop. (Why were we doing this again?) Those with an ice pick can dig into the snow and slow the descent some. We had none. As crazy as it sounds, it can be a lot of fun, if one lives to tell about it.

Not everyone was game for this. Some carefully descended down steps dug in the snow, or went around the edge on the boulders. Daniel and Brooks went flying down the several hundred-foot snowfield first, stopping before the rocky bottom by digging their heels into the snow. They stood to cheer their own accomplishment, received our applause, and then waved us on.

I went next, flailing all the way down, uselessly grabbing at snow, turning circles, and trying not to scream. I was able to right myself, dig in my heels near the bottom, and roll to a stop before the rocks. Barely.

Cedric stood at the top, waiting for the sign to abandon caution and slide on down. He clearly wanted to do this. I've got to give him kudos for courage. The three of us really didn't think he should try glissading here and tried to shout that up to him. I waved him off, but, much to our surprise, he must have seen this as the "go" sign and launched himself into the slick groove that the three of us had created.

"Whoa, whoa, whoa!" we all reacted in chorus.

Cedric came speeding down at me, the bulk of him barely fitting into the impression we had made, accelerating all the more with the snow packed down from our runs. I stood, jaw agape, watching the impending train wreck charging towards me. My back was to the rocks, and here came Cedric totally out of control, arms and legs flailing, turning circles in the slide, rolling, readjusting himself, and snow-plowing great plumes all around him.

As I observed this, in real, but seeming slow-motion time, it wasn't as if my life was passing before me; it was more like visualizing my impending doom, either by being clobbered into a coma upon impact, or being carried into and mangled by the ancient glacier-produced debris field. Neither option appealed to me.

I processed my choices—all in a split second. Leaping out of the way didn't seem very heroic. I had invited Cedric to come on this adventure with us, so I had a certain responsibility to get him home, and in one piece. And he had a wife and children at home, awaiting his safe return. I had to try *something*.

This was crazy. Cedric had a 100-pound advantage on me. He was barreling down the mountain at a speed that would have qualified him to make the Olympic bobsled team, or to *be* the bobsled. Some vague recollection of high school physics—momentum, moving object vs. stationary object, and all that—told me I wasn't in a very good place.

I determined that timing was everything. He'd be on me in a moment. I caught his expression: I couldn't quite tell if it was a huge grin or a grimace. Daniel and Brooks rushed to join me in the rescue, or dead body removal.

I moved up some from the rocks and dug my boots into the snow. A microsecond before impact, I dove forward. Driving my shoulder into the snow underneath him, like some kind of a football body block, I tried to create a wedge to stop Cedric's chaotic slide. As we collided, my move slowed his momentum, but barely.

My feet pushed out of their footholds, and now we were both sliding towards the sharp-edged rocks. Cedric had turned sideways, and I was afraid he was going to roll right over me. I fought to hold on to him as I tried to gain foot traction. Daniel and Brooks jumped on the both of us, dragging their boot toes in the snow like anchors, and rode us to a safe stop. We all sat up, covered in sloppy snow, red-faced, breathing heavily, and laughing so hard we had to wipe our eyes with our soaking-wet gloves.

By the time we reached the SUV, the sun had warmed the day back up again through a clear blue sky. It was as if the snowstorm had never occurred. Cedric felt better, and was grateful for what he was able to do. Daniel had climbed farther and higher than he'd ever done before. Nobody died. This had been a good day.

It was a day that none of us will ever forget. We endured the climb, braved the unexpected harsh elements, conquered a 14er in extreme conditions, survived our glissading adventure, and saw Cedric's prayers answered. We left no man behind, lived to tell this tale, and to climb another day.

A collection of memories can be made deliberately, accidentally, or circumstantially. Shared memories and storytelling of our times together make us an affinity group, a community, a family. It gives us a place where we *belong*.

This account will be told amongst ourselves, recounted to our *tribes*, and to others, for years to come. Our story from this weekend is layered, and is interwoven into other stories: Daniel's safe return from overseas combat duty, and his kind welcome home; his and Cedric's first 14er attempt; Bob's last 14er; fathers and sons bonding together; friendships deepened; challenges met and personal victories accomplished.

Should we have attempted all that we tried to do? Was it safe? Wise? Maybe not. Judgment calls were made. And it turned out okay.

This is not an outdoor activity for everyone. And one doesn't have to put oneself in jeopardy to have a wonderful wilderness time. For us, this was the stuff of great adventure, marvelous fellowship, and lasting memories. Out of the sometimes dull routine of our workaday lives, we were, at least for one day, truly *alive*. And none of us would have traded that for the world.

Marching On!

Colorado Trail Segment 8, Tennessee Pass to Camp Hale

"... the result was that they accomplished the impossible."

— Field Marshall Bernard Montgomery —

Poor Diane was down again. This time upside down. Barely visible above the edge of the snow hole that had swallowed her, her snowshoes were kicking skywards, pleading for solid ground again. Although Kevin and I, and my inverted, squirming wife had "post-holed" hundreds of times already on this Colorado Trail segment, in less-than-ideal snow pack, no one had actually been engulfed up whole, until now.

"A little help here, boys" a muffled voice patiently pleaded from behind us. What a trooper!

Each of us had fought the snow that day. It wasn't so bad on the trail through the forest. But out in the open meadows, the conditions for snowshoeing were horrible. We'd take one step, sink into another hole, pull that foot out, and take another step, only to repeat the laborious process all over again.

Kevin and Diane review map on Colorado trail to keep us on course, post holing and all.

We all struggled, but no one wanted to quit. Going was ridiculously slow (to say the least!), fatiguing, and just seemed impossible. Every step plunged each of us into an unknown cavity and subsequent attempt to escape. Once, earlier on in the hike, Diane had called to us, and when we turned, we saw her waist-deep in snow that had collapsed in on her. When Kevin and I pulled her out, one of her snowshoes came off, and we had to dig deep to retrieve it.

There are reasons that most people don't hike the CT in winter. Deep snow at an elevation of over 10,000 ft.—now, we, in exhaustion, admitted—was definitely one of those reasons. We had divided up the long Segment 8 into two parts and had come back to finish the latter half snowshoeing. The hike trended mostly downhill from Tennessee Pass to just past historic Camp Hale. Snowdrifts that looked solid enough ended up just being a thin, frozen crust that broke away near buried willow bushes, and left us thigh-deep in snow, or worse.

"Any time now!" Diane entreated from inside the icy cavity.

Although Kevin and I did find this sight terribly amusing (and simply had to take one photo), we did pull Diane out, spitting snow. We trudged forward together. We would leave no trail soldier behind! She appreciated that.

Trail's End for us was Camp Hale at 9,200 feet. This unique military base—really, an entire town—was built in 1942 to train troops for high altitude and winter warfare during WWII. The 10th Mt. Division learned cold weather survival, rock climbing, rappelling, and downhill skiing, along with standard basic training, before heading out to Europe to fight the Germans in Italy's Apennine Mountains.

The division faced brutal mountain combat conditions at Riva Ridge. The German army considered the ridge to be impossible to climb, and undermanned the fortifications. The 10th scaled a 1,500 ft. ascent for a surprise nighttime assault. After taking Riva Ridge, Mt. Belvedere was the next offensive. This peak was heavily manned and protected with minefields.

Soldiers from the 10th Division made a bayonet attack without artillery fire cover. Again, the surprise of the assault was successful and, following a hard fight, the mountain defenses were captured.

Realizing the importance of the peak, the German army made seven counterattacks over two days. The intense combat at Riva Ridge and Mt. Belvedere left the Americans with 850 casualties, including 195 dead. But the 10th had captured 1,000 prisoners, and the Americans were now in a position to breach the German's Apennine Mountain line, and open the way to the Po Valley.

The 10th spearheaded the attacks against the Germans all the way to the River Po in the spring of 1945. Casualties were heavy. General Mark Clark called the 10th the greatest unit ever to fight in Italy. And British Field Marshall Montgomery had this to say: "The only trouble with the 10th Mountain Division was that the officers and men did not realize that they were attempting something that couldn't be done, and after they started they had too much intestinal fortitude to quit. The result was that they accomplished the impossible."

In his diary of events with the 10th Mountain Division during the war, Harris Dusenbury recounted what America already knew: the 10th were heroic and victorious. He writes, "Our hearts went out to the 992 that died. We faced enemy artillery, mortar fire, small arms fire and crossed fields with mines in the thousands. We advanced with stealth and with verve and daring. We lost only twelve as prisoners, but our wounded numbered 3,849 ... during the 114 days we were engaged in Italy. We took the high ground and we always held it."

Former Senator and presidential candidate Bob Dole was one of those seriously wounded. On April 15, 1945, Dole, a lieutenant and a replacement, was ordered to lead an ambush patrol outside of Castel d'Aiano in the Apennine Mountains, southwest of Bologna. He was hit by German machine gun fire in his upper right back and his right arm was also badly injured. When fellow soldiers saw the extent of his injuries, all they thought they could do was to give him the largest dose of morphine they dared, and then write an "M" for morphine on his forehead in his own blood, so that no one else who found him would give him a second, fatal dose. Dole was decorated three times, receiving two Purple Hearts for his injuries, and the Bronze Star with combat "V" for valor for his attempt to assist a downed radioman.

The three of us walked through the former Camp Hale in reverence. Silence surrounded us, except for the gentle rustle of the meadow grass from a light breeze. Not much remains of the town today except some concrete foundations, a bit of twisted rebar, and a memorial plaque on Tennessee Pass commemorating the sacrifice of the 10th. Looking at the little that is left of the base, it's hard to believe that, at one time, 15,000 people, 5,000 mules, and 200 dogs lived here. Camp Hale was abandoned in 1963 and subsequently demolished. One short row of bunker walls, spared for historical value, sits beside the Eagle River.

The river here looks odd and unnatural with its arrow-straight course through what used to be the base. When building the camp, the army bulldozed its channel to conform to the orderly grid of the town's streets. There are plans to restore the Eagle back to the meandering, meadow trout stream it once was.

We stumbled, sore and tired, but grateful and satisfied, up to our awaiting truck. Given the Mountain Division's WWII battles, severe hardships, and heavy casualties, I could hardly complain about our arduous little snow hike. We did march on, helped each over the challenging terrain, dug one another out, and encouraged ourselves to keep our eyes on the goal. We learned about the history of the region and about the sacrifices of others for our freedoms. What more could we want from a winter snowshoe hike along the Colorado Trail?

Well, maybe fewer holes.

Revenge of the Old Man on the Mountain

Huron Peak, Handies Peak, Colorado

"If someone throws a stone at you, throw a flower at them. But remember to throw the flower pot with it."

— Unknown —

My friend Bob McCrea had never climbed a fourteener. One would think that with my experience, I would make a good selection for a first-timer. A mountain, perhaps, that was a little easier (comparatively speaking), one that had a strong trail, was well maintained, and had shorter round-trip mileage. One would *think*.

I suppose, at the time, in my own twisted defense, I was continuing to make errors in judgment in such cases based on my drive to continue to "bag" peaks I had not yet climbed. I didn't want to go backwards and summit an easier peak that I had climbed before. Unfortunately, many of my high-altitude guests over the years suffered unnecessarily as a result.

Bob was a fit man in his 60's. A gentleman rancher from Minnesota, he rode horses, participated in fox hunts, worked his property, went on long bike rides, downhill skied in Colorado, and had hiked many times above tree line. But climbing a 14,000 ft. mountain is quite another physical feat.

What started out for us as a business associate relationship had turned into a warm friendship. When Bob would visit Colorado for business, he, my best buddy, Bruce, and I would always catch dinner together. We'd discuss the "stuff of life" late into the evening, and tip the restaurant server well for staying so long. Despite our differences in age, Bob's young-at-heart attitude and zest for life made him seem like "just one of the guys." I suspect (in hindsight) that our decision to climb a 14er together tested Bob's commitment to the relationship.

We had planned the trip weeks in advance. I made sure that Bob brought a well-stocked daypack with him, having provided him with an essential list of 14er climbing supplies. I had also encouraged Bob to do what he could before coming out—even going on local hikes where he lived—to get into climbing shape. Bruce was joining us, and had climbed with me before, so he knew the routine, and the risks with hiking with me.

Our adventure started the night before with lodging in the old mining town of Leadville. We stayed at the historic Delaware Hotel, a charming Western-Victorian Inn built in 1886. We may have slept in the same rooms where Doc Holiday, Harry Houdini, or the Unsinkable Molly Brown had stayed. At this scenic elevation of 10,152 feet, The Delaware is the highest hotel in the United States. The prime rib dinner at a local restaurant was exceptional. Carnivores all, no pasta meals or frou-frou salads for us!

We got up before dawn and our anticipation increased on our drive the closer we got to the foothills of the Northern Sawatch Mountain Range. Into the mountains on a bumpy 4-wheel-drive road, we passed through the well-preserved mining ghost town of Winfield. Even with our early start, the trailhead parking lot was crowded.

I had chosen Huron Peak (14,003 ft.) for Bob's first fourteener. On the standard, well-groomed trail, this is a popular peak for large groups and families with older children, and lots of dogs. I opted to have us climb a more difficult route. This probably explained why we saw no one going the direction of our intended trail.

Before we started out, I had the guys do stretching exercises, then we all had a small energy snack. We kick-started our climb with good hydration. We watched in curiosity as a group loaded supplies on pack llamas. I was aware of this type of hiking in Colorado, especially with multi-day backpacking trips, but had not seen it done before. As cute as they were, I had heard that llamas like to spit at you, so I kept my distance.

The start of our climb took us up a beautiful valley, and gave us spectacular views of the Three Apostles, a close chain of three peaks, with Ice Mountain in the middle, which is considered one of the most difficult peaks to summit in Colorado. My flawed plan was deliberately *not* to take the traditional route, like the more sensible crowds with children and dogs did, but to hike up the valley to the starting point of a moderate rising ridge. The ridge traverse eventually meets up with the last, and steeper, ascent section to the summit of Huron Peak. We could then descend the nice, gentle, meadow and forest switchbacks of the conventional way down. This brilliant strategy may have worked okay had I just stuck to the plan.

Impatient to get to the toothy ridge sooner, I made a hard left way too early, thereby starting us up a very steep, rocky slope instead of traveling farther and following the beginning of the gentler ridge trail. Any hope of a path up this difficult rockslide area quickly disappeared—we were on our own, trail blazing where no man or spitting llama had gone before.

The talus became wobbly, the climb steeper, our pace much slower, as we tried to negotiate our way up the dangerous incline. No sharp-edged boulder could be trusted to bear our weight and not throw us sideways into another rock with similar malicious intent. The mountain fought back every step as we attempted to conquer it. It wasn't going down without a fight.

The incline at this point was nearly 45 degrees. I looked back at Bob and Bruce spidering hand and foot in a slow uphill crawl. All the eager enthusiasm and cheerful smiles from the morning had left them, only to be replaced with a combined expression of exhaustion and dismay (probably mixed with a little anger at their team leader for taking them this way). I kept my short distance from them in case murder crossed their minds.

Bruce was doing fairly well, but Bob was looking ill, breathing heavily, and pouring sweat like a fire hose. His red face was now turning green—not a good color on anyone at this altitude. He stalled frequently (much of that was to be expected climbing a 14er), as he grumbled, or swore something unintelligible at his *former* good friend, Tim. He then finally stopped altogether. He sat on a see-saw boulder, trying without much success to catch his breath and regain his composure, and looked to see if there was any way he could turn back—but not before beating me unconscious with his hiking stick. (Honestly, he would not have done that ... he was just too tired.)

I have a progressive approach to helping myself when struggling on a mountain like this, which intensifies when I'm responsible for others. When flat out lying to encourage or fool others doesn't work (as in, "Not much farther, Guys," or "It's just around the bend," or blatantly misleading "We're almost there!"), I start with increased hydration, a high-energy snack, and a short bit of rest. As needed, we move to an electrolyte drink or an energy-boost jolt like a Red Bull drink. These tactics applied to Bob got him another 100 yards or so—preserving my life for the moment—but he stopped again, and this time I thought for good.

I knew I had to bring out the BIG stuff. I rummaged into the bottom of my pack and retrieved the emergency rescue energy solution, the GU. Hard to describe, it tastes something like a combination of paste glue and fruity snail slime. Understand, I'm only imagining, at least about the snail slime, and I hadn't had paste glue since the third grade. But, powerful and fast acting, GU was the last resort to get Bob up to the ridge, then to the top.

He balked as I gently held his head up off his chest and squeezed the orange sludge into his mouth. He almost gagged, and threatened to spit it back on me like a llama, but Bruce and I pressured him to swallow it. He took it like medicine, and like a man. He may have thought this was some kind of torturous, sick joke on our parts, but I really did have his best interests in mind. I knew how much this trip meant to him, and how he so wanted us to summit together.

After a short while, Bob perked up as we'd hoped. I'm sure he didn't know what was worse: the sheer exhaustion of the climb, or swallowing the fruititious (my word, marketing folks, royalties expected) GU mud, which made him feel more ill, but energized at the same time. Up, up up, we slowly crawled, as I encouraged Bob one rocky, wobbly stumble-step at a time.

We did reach the jagged ridge, and slowly worked our way to the summit. As we each stepped onto the small top, high fives, hearty back pats and manly hugs of joy followed. Bob had climbed his first 14er! We signed the register, took dozens of photos, gobbled down a quick snack lunch, and were ready to start our descent.

There was no way I was taking the guys back down the way we came. We were all too spent to try that challenge on the return. I had always planned to descend the easier standard route. What a difference this well-maintained trail was! Gentle slopes, undemanding switchbacks, built-in stairs, graded paths, all made clear as to why it was the recommended trail. We came upon a large group of volunteers working hard to make the already agreeable path even more pleasant!

As we moved through a section of lush green high alpine meadows, one of the young people working the trail with a pick ax yelled over to us, "Hey, did you guys see the Old Man of the Mountain?" Not understanding her meaning, both Bruce and I teasingly looked over at Bob and asked, "Is she talking about you?"

"No, over here," she motioned, and directed our gaze to scattered blooms of flowering plants, ones we might have missed completely without her catching our attention.

We were told we had the opportunity to view quite a rare treat: the Old Man of the Mountain flower. How we overlooked this beautiful, yellow, daisy-like flower—in stark contrast to the other alpine tundra—must have said something about how tired we were. The flowers were so large that they nearly obscured their stem and leaves. We learned that this plant can only be found above the treeline (12,000 ft.) and that it only blooms once in seven years! This was truly special!

We made it back to our car in one piece, or in Bob's case, perhaps several pieces held together with GU. He had survived his first big adventure with us … and, amazingly, it wouldn't be his last. I guess that's the stuff of trust and friendship.

○ ○ ○

One year later, our good friend, and good sport, Bob, climbed another fourteener with Bruce and me. This was a little hard to believe after the Huron Peak Debacle, as it came to be called, but he was game for an additional mountain summit. I chose Handies Peak (14,048 ft.). I had assured him that this next one would be easier (surprisingly, he believed me).

We left Colorado Springs after lunch to drive to Lake City, a historic mining town established in 1885. We enjoy the long drives together, and our dinners out, just about as much as our wilderness experiences. I dominated our usual round-table transit discussions telling the guys about writing a new novel that was a supernatural thriller. I think I creeped Bob out a little with too many scary details, making him unsure he really wanted to spend the night in the same mountain cabin with me. I assured him that was an alter ego, and that the one he was with was safe … well, safe enough.

I had researched lodging and we agreed to stay at the G&M Cabins. This charming, rustic and unique cabin complex, centered in the old downtown district, sat in contrast to the other classy Victorian "Pink Lady" B&B lodging in town, and was a perfect start of our next adventure. We stayed in a small, red cabin that was built in the late 1800s. After a fabulous steak dinner, with a bottle of cabernet sauvignon, at an unexpectedly cosmopolitan restaurant, with fresh-cut flowers on the table, we stayed up too late in our cozy cabin discussing the things of real importance to us. This was beginning to feel more like a women's retreat than a manly outing. But it was good to get in touch with our sensitive sides.

Up before dawn, we downed energy bars, double-checked our packs, and started gulping down the water. Our drive up the American Basin rugged 4-wheel drive trail was beautiful, but challenging, as we crossed several swollen streams. The views looking up from our parking spot, past a huge bowl at the base of Handies Peak were awe-inspiring. This spectacular view alone would have made the whole trip worth it, but we had a mountain to summit as well.

This climb—really qualifying as a *hike*—was much shorter and more moderate than our Huron challenge. After summit congratulations, our own "elevation celebration," we surveyed the 360-degree panoramic surroundings. The sunny conditions on top were wonderful. Seldom on my 14er climbs am I able to sit for a while in the warm sun, enjoy the clear views and have lunch—this day was the exception. Typically, it is ridiculously cold on top, with high winds announcing the coming threat of a cold front moving fast toward me, with snow or hail in its wake.

On past climbs, I have had to quickly sign the register, take a couple of photos, and get off the summit immediately—no time for sightseeing, if I want to live to climb another day. I asked a fellow once, coming up a mountain in such terrible conditions, in shorts, with no pack, and carrying only a small disposable water bottle, if he'd like to leave me a phone number to contact next of kin. He just grunted passing me. Oh, well. To each his own, short, life.

On our way back down Handies, we passed close to the crystal-clear, high-altitude lake that we had seen on the way up. I asked Bruce, "Do you want to make a memory today?"

"What … do … you … mean?" he returned with a knowing look, eyebrow raised.

"It's hot out. We're here," I said. "Let's take a cool dunk."

"Not in *there*!"

"Come on! We're sweaty, and dusty. It will feel great!" I lied.

There was no way Bob was going in, but he encouraged us to take the jump into the freezing water. "I'll act as official photographer," he said.

After some pondering, with more than a little hesitation, Bruce finally agreed to take the plunge with me. How bad could it be, really? I imagined how refreshing, how wonderfully invigorating, this dip would feel.

Bruce and I stripped out of our hiking boots and clothes down to our skivvies. Bruce is still in very good shape for his middle age, not that I was paying that close attention. I, on the other hand, was trying very hard to hold my stomach in, feeling all of six months preggers, with still no name for the baby. Bob held the camera at the ready.

With tighty-whities gleaming in the bright sunshine, we did the 1-2-3 count, ran from the small sandy shore, and leapt into the drink. I thought I knew the meaning of cold, but this stupid decision redefined the word. It was nothing less than shocking.

We splashed forward a few yards, expecting the shoreline to drop off more quickly. Both of us found that high-pitched shrieking like women momentarily helped with the intense pain. (No offense meant to shrieking women out there.) But the freezing cold water got the best of us and took our breath away. It felt as if thousands of needles pricked our skin, and our muscles immediately constricted.

"Go out a little farther!" Bob shouted, as he tracked us through the viewfinder. "Let's get you with your heads just above the water. It will look great!" We barely could think, or move, but wanted to cooperate for the photographic record.

"H-h-hurry," we spat out.

"A little farther out! Just a little farther! Okay, I got it!"

We flailed wildly back to shore (hard to call it swimming), yelling unintelligible phrases as our blue lips stopped working. We stumbled up onto the beach and fell onto our hands and knees, shivering uncontrollably. We looked to Bob for affirmation that he had captured the torturous moments.

"I didn't get it!" Bob exclaimed from a short distance away. We stared at him in disbelief, bright red as the blood rushed back to the surface of our skin.

"W-w-what? H-h-how?" we both stuttered.

"Something happened with the camera! It seems to be working now! You are going to have to do it again ... if you want this documented!"

Bruce and I looked at each other, grimacing, covered with goose bumps. We *did* want to record this foolish undertaking, but would it be worth it to put ourselves through that agony again? With a reluctant nod, we stood to prepare ourselves for another frigid dunking. Whose idea was this again? We turned away from Bob as our briefs became quite translucent when wet.

"Ready?" we asked Bob. He gave us the thumbs up, and I thought I saw a little impish smile come from the corner of his mouth from behind the camera.

After the repeat frenetic splashing and screaming, we looked back to see Bob doubled over in hilarity, not even photographing the epic event. We realized that we had been had! We forced our stone-stiff arms and legs in a jerky, zombie-like motion back to shore.

Bob couldn't stop laughing. Bruce and I joined in the merriment of Bob's hijinks, through chattering teeth. We figured this was payback for the tough Huren climb, the force-fed GU, and the "Old Man of the Mountain" ribbing. We were right. At least we had the photos to prove our mettle, and memories of fun and good friendships for a lifetime.

Two Tickets to Paradise

Windom Peak, Sunlight Peak, South Mount Eolus, Chicago Basin, San Juan Mountains, CO

Doubly happy, however, is the man to whom lofty mountain-tops are within reach.

— John Muir —

Someone asked me the other day what my favorite hike was. That is difficult to answer because I have had so many wonderful wilderness experiences. I would tend to divide them into categories: the desert solitude; shadowed canyons; lush meadows or woodlands; high alpine, with waterfalls and pristine lakes; or climbs up 14,000 ft. peaks. So, how do I narrow the choice to just one? If pressed, I may have to say my favorite was my hike into the Chicago Basin in the San Juan Mountains, and the summit of three of the most remote 14er peaks.

We spent the night before our extraordinary time in the mountains in Durango, Colorado. Kevin and I lugged our backpacks onto the beds in the hotel room. They were double-heavy as we had strapped day packs on as well, intending to use them instead of the big packs for our climbs. I had not backpacked since college, and being older now, felt I needed more "creature comforts," and so had filled the packs to capacity and beyond with "necessities."

Kevin laughed uncontrollably when I heaved my pack on, and promptly fell backwards onto the bed from the weight of it. Strapped in, and unable to move, Kevin had to come over and unhitch me. This was ridiculous.

Tales from the Trails

Neither of us had invested in the ultra-lite gear. The trip to our campsite was several miles up a rugged, steep trail from the Needleton Trailhead. No way were we going to try to pack that much weight. So we began to strip items out of the backpacks that we felt we could do without. Gone was the solar-powered TV, the king size mattress, the inflatable hot tub, and the La-Z-Boy recliner. Seriously, we eliminated about 20 pounds each from our packs. We would not have to rent pack mules, or spitting llamas.

We had purchased our train tickets on-line, in advance, to guarantee a seat. This is the very popular narrow gauge, coal-fired, steam locomotive tourist attraction that runs along the Animas River from Durango to the old mining town of Silverton. The train drops backpackers off about halfway up. You can imagine our enthusiasm as the vintage locomotive whistle blew and we jerked forward in our passenger car, the plume of engine smoke billowing overhead. We were pumped as the train wound its way through the breathtaking canyons of the San Juan National Forest, spitting coal grapple back at us through the open windows.

Off the train, our gusto waned about half way up the 6-mile hike, 3,000 vertical foot drainage of Needle Creek to High Camp at 10,900 feet, our staging area. Both Kevin and I wished we'd left another 20 pounds of "stuff" back at the car. My buckling legs felt like they would completely give out, forcing me to crawl on all fours the rest of the way. I wobbled forward, taking frequent rest breaks where I could lean the pack on a tree or boulder. Other athletic hikers with cool, lightweight gear, dressed in the latest brightly-colored trekking fashions, blew past us with mixed reactions of sympathy and snickers. Then, it started to rain. And rain. And rain.

We reached our destination in the lower Chicago Basin cirque, set up camp in a damp, small grove of pines, and prepared our well-earned, freeze-dried dinner. Yum—my favorite! The rain took a break for a short while, and with the remaining light of the day, we decided to take a reconnaissance hike. When we headed out in the morning, in the dark, we wanted to have a good sense of our way.

The trail had become more of a creek. We hiked up a headwall to a shelf at 11,600 feet overlooking the huge bowl that is Chicago Basin. I can't begin to describe the surrounding beauty of this place—words alone fall short of doing it justice. Craggy rock monoliths bit into the sky. Lush emerald grasses and shrubs blanketed the valley, punctuated by boulders and groves of evergreens. Streams flowed from every direction, headwaters of Needle Creek.

Shards of the last light stabbed through the clouds mottling the landscape. A small herd of mountain goats surrounded us, unthreatened by our presence. I slowly turned 360 degrees to try to take in the splendor. I counted eleven significant waterfalls pouring into the basin. This was a privilege beyond compare that both humbles and uplifts the spirit. Washington Irving said it well: "There is a serene and settled majesty to woodland scenery that enters into the soul and delights and elevates it, and fills it with noble inclinations." Kevin and I were silent before the majestic scene that unfolded around us. Mountain grandeur.

"My father considered a walk among the mountains as the equivalent of churchgoing," Aldous Huxley writes. What is church? Surely, more than a building. Certainly a place where God dwells. In people. In nature. If so, then this was church.

Low clouds built up and blanketed the landscape, tucking the peaks in for the evening. Back to our tent, Kevin and I read paperbacks by lantern light. It rained through most of the night, hard at times, which was both strangely soothing, and unsettling.

○ ○ ○

Our early morning was chilly, dark, sloppy wet ... and exhilarating! The promise of adventure hung in the air like the moisture from the rain. After a quick breakfast bar and a hot cup of tea, we grabbed our daypacks, put on our headlamps, and were off. Our reconnoiter from the previous evening paid off in setting our general direction, but the path was mostly opaque in the pitch black, and we sloshed through puddles and mud.

Regaining the shelf, we followed a climbing traverse to Twin Lakes, and from there, scrambled up to another basin below the northwest face of Windom Peak. With the continued overcast, the grey dawn didn't bring the expected yellow-red alpenglow to the peaks. We knew that frequent, severe weather in Chicago Basin was to be expected—South Mt. Eolus is named for The Greek god of the wind, no doubt a reference to the fast approaching storms that hit this region. We hoped the weather would hold for us.

By the time we reached a 13,240 ft. saddle, and then began climbing up Windom's West Ridge, heavy torrents started up again and we put on our rain gear. Summiting, we had to make a decision. Most climbers would turn back at this point. Most should. We should have. 14ers are difficult enough when dry. When wet, they pose an additional crazy-dangerous challenge.

Here's the deal (and our wives can quit reading now): neither Kevin nor I are reckless, or have a death wish. Each of us, at one point, has left our quest for a peak summit for a later time due to inclement weather. But we had made these plans months in advance, driven a full day to get to Durango, had inhaled train smoke for two hours (and paid $50 each for the privilege), piggy-backed roughly our own weight in our backpacks six miles up hill, set up base in the rain, and had climbed up into this high basin above our camp not once, but twice! No way were we coming back another day!

We pressed on to peak number two, carefully working our way over slick rock, down the ridge to a midway point that looked good to traverse over to a gully—the only non-technical route up Sunlight Peak. Slipping and sliding over wet, loose scree, we slowly made our way to our second summit via another steep ridge. The true summit for Sunlight is a huge boulder, separated by a deep crack. To climb it requires a Class 4 bouldering move that meant jumping the crevasse and immediately running up the 45-degree angle to grab the top edge and hang on. Getting down was even more difficult. We decided, in the pouring rain, that our summit point was good enough to count the peak as "bagged."

Whereas Windom and Sunlight were somewhat "connected," Eolus looked far off. Back down to Twin Lakes, and at the lower elevation, the rain let up a bit. This was a nice break. Rain gear really doesn't keep one dry, just *less wet*. At the base of South Mount Eolus, I hit a wall, figuratively speaking. This had been a tough day—both physically and mentally, with the heightened attention to the dicey conditions—and it wasn't over for us yet. We had to complete South Mount Eolus, and at that time. The next day, Sunday, needed to be a travel-home day. I had to be back to work Monday morning. Kevin and I sat for a few minutes to recoup, rehydrating and forcing down energy bars. In a short time, we were moving again, determined to complete our goal.

Ascending was slow, due to both our exhaustion and the difficult scramble up the couloir between North Mount Eolus (not an official 14er) and South Mount Eolus. We climbed back into cloud cover again. Just before we reached the steep rock ridge that connects the two peaks, we saw something that neither of us had ever seen in all our years of hiking.

What first caught our attention was a bright-blue backpack on the ground. Evidently, a climber ahead of us had stripped off the weight for his final push to the top. We would *never* be caught without our packs, but could understand his or her need to lighten the load for the summit. So there was this pack, separated from its owner … and *slowly moving*.

As we cautiously approached, we saw a large yellow-bellied marmot trying its best to drag the pack into its burrow within a rock pile. We both laughed out loud, which the marmot ignored while continuing his determined tugging, with some unlikely success. It must have thought that this was fortuitous blessing from above! How often does this happen in a marmot's lifetime? Food dropped special delivery at its door, and with den stuffing materials for hibernation-warmth through the wintertime! I felt a bit sorry for it as we chased it away with claps and shouts. We warned the pack's original owner, on his way down off the top, that he'd better hurry if he wanted to see his possessions again.

Halfway back to camp—after Kevin had accidentally bent his hiking stick in half between two large rocks—the sun broke through the dissipating clouds; its day-end shout to let the region know it hadn't permanently gone on vacation. Waning golden light warmed not just our bodies, but also our souls. We did some housekeeping and packing, then we just collapsed into the tent. Our long day would be followed by an early morning.

We were told to take seriously the warning that the train would not wait for the returning backpackers, so we should have gotten an earlier start back down the canyon. Approaching the stop, the engineer would start blowing his whistle. The train would arrive promptly at 2:00 p.m. and depart immediately after loading the backpacks and hikers. If you missed the train, you could plan on camping at the stop until the next day—an option neither of us could afford.

Sure enough, a few minutes before 2:00 we heard the horn blow in a distant canyon, while we were still making our way to the trailhead pick-up area! We began running the last half mile or so—with those heavy packs on! We were glad to see the train had not departed before we arrived, as a few remaining hikers were still loading up.

We had done it—even if it was somewhat dumb. Three 14ers in one day could be rough enough, and we had decided to do it in the rain. We felt we had to. Now, we did not have to come back again to Chicago basin, unless we wanted to. I would love to return one day, even if just to camp in this little piece of heaven—a true, high-altitude paradise.

Best Laid Plans

Canyonlands, Island in the Sky, Moab, Utah

"It was amazing how you could get so far from where you'd planned, and yet find it exactly where you needed to be."

— Sarah Dessen, What happened to Goodbye —

I plan my adventure hiking trips down to the finest details. Why wouldn't I? I want to pack as much into one, two or three days in the wilderness as is inhumanly possible. So, I create a tight schedule, with a plethora of activities, and one that runs from dawn to dusk. If I'm a tour guide for friends or family, I hope they'll appreciate the planning effort I've put in. Most hate it, but they're shortsighted.

For some reason, those who accompany me on an outing think I will provide a relaxing time, safe adventure, full of casual sightseeing, kept at a leisurely pace, with easy trekking and plenty of opportunities to stop and photograph the cactuses. What a concept! With so much to see and do in the great outdoors, one simply *has* to force-fit as much activity into a trip as time allows, right?

And, did I have an agenda for my friends and writers' group buddies, Gino Martinelli (Gene) and Ray Seldomridge. It was their first trip out to Moab, and I had to show them *everything* there was to see and do over a three-day weekend one March.

It had taken Kevin and me several years to try to cover the many miles of rugged trials around this scenic marvel of southeast Utah. And there is still more for us to tackle. I had so much to show Gene and Ray. I would run them ragged, and the beauty of the place would knock their socks off! That's what a good tour guide does. They'd be exhausted and barefoot when I was through with them, or I hadn't done my job. They would thank me later.

Our little writers' group had spent countless hours reading, critiquing, and editing each other's work. A weekend retreat for defining creative priorities, encouraging each other in this punishing effort, and inspiring them in the breathtaking nature trail hiking seemed like a grand idea. And, we all needed a break from our workaday routines.

The Friday afternoon, seven-hour drive to Moab seemed to fly by as we rapid-fire discussed our current writing projects, the nature of why and how we write, the challenges of getting an imaginative idea out of our heads and onto the computer screen, the frustrations and discouragements of the process, the despair of ever getting published, and whether that even mattered. We took a break from this heady conversation to have dinner along the way at my favorite brewery-restaurant in Glenwood Springs—one that I had handpicked in advance for their enjoyment. I'm surprised I didn't order for them as well, and cut up their food, just to keep things moving.

We arrived late, and had a good night's sleep at the Red Cliff Lodge along the Colorado River, outside of Moab. We woke early, shared in a reading from the Desert Fathers (a third-century monastic movement in Northern Africa—seriously, good stuff) and *planned* our day, meaning that I told the guys what they'd be doing.

At breakfast in the Moab Diner, Gene and Ray might have fit in well as locals. They were dressed appropriately for outdoor adventures. Big Ray (he's 6' 15" or something) looked the part of the writer-philosopher-desert-hermit, perhaps reminding one of the prickly wilderness essayist, Edward Abbey. Gene sported a large salt-and-pepper beard, wore a plaid shirt and big boots, and looked all the part of a jovial desert prospector who comes into town for some decent grub two or three times a year. I, on the other hand, with my long face, pasty-white complexion (I'm so white I could get a moonburn; so white, in fact, I'm almost transparent), a shock of bright red hair, a big allergy-ridden pink nose, with my goofy, giant broad-brimmed hat (my personal, wearable umbrella), must have looked like the circus had arrived in town.

I had planned for a fun writer's exercise during breakfast. Just enjoying the meal simply wasn't enough. We could take that time to pack something else in. The guys were game. We would each (discretely, not in a creepy way) select a patron in the diner, take notes, come up with a story concept, and we would later write about that person. (Okay, now it does sound kinda creepy.)

I had determined—okay, planned—that on an outdoors lunch break, we'd take some time to reflect on the beauty, and start to flesh out our stories. Gene took his story a theatrical direction exposing a feud between two Moab residents, and very cleverly wrote it as a segment for a screenplay. Ray imagined, with his insightful flair, a couple's conversation filled with stealth and intrigue, driven by a spiritual awakening and a dramatic flight from a former life. My run at a story is an add-on at the end of this chapter, if you'd care to read it. The jury is still out on whether I can write fiction—although, some would argue that parts of my stories in this book are fiction.

It was at the end of the meal—as I was showing the guys an Excel spreadsheet of the full schedule I hoped to accomplish that day, the region we'd cover, the miles of hiking we'd traverse—when they announced they were both nursing painful foot ailments and so were interested mostly in short hikes, rather than the kind of transcontinental journeys written up in *National Geographic*. "Short hikes"? I had planned this whole trip around getting these guys *far* out into the wilderness!

This just couldn't be! Gene had an ingrown toenail; Ray was struggling with plantar fasciitis on one heel. I had expressly instructed them in the weeks leading up to this expedition to stay healthy, and to get into good shape. And now this? Didn't they know how much work I had put into the planning of this trip—for *their* enjoyment?

And, they continued, nearly in unison, that they were fine with walking *near* the edge of cliffs, but that *teetering over* the edge of said cliffs did not have much appeal. "Tightrope acts should stay in the circus," Ray said.

What was going on here? Did they not know of the rugged region around Moab, with all its outdoor activities, and the nature of the exploration there? Surely I had shared my past experiences enough with them. Everything here is either several hundred feet up, or several hundred feet down!

Now what was I going to do with these guys? They couldn't hike much, couldn't climb up anything, and couldn't walk along the edge of any precipice. Oh, and they insisted that we not drive on any steep off-road dirt trails, without railings, like the infamous Shafer Trail. I think one of them said derisively, "Mr. Tim's Wild Ride? Been there, done that at Disneyland." But they were still eagerly anticipating a wonderful time here, and looked to their tour guide to provide it.

I had to be fast on my (good) feet. Yes, I could plan a revised itinerary on a moment's notice. I had been out to Moab so many times that I could customize an experience for these limping, phobic, first-timers. In the past, I had created for others my "Taste of Moab" two-day journey and the "Moab Experience," a three-day excursion, but I could quickly come up with the "Gimps and Wimps" car tour. It wouldn't be the trip that *I* wanted to go on, but it could be done. I didn't even consider *their* disappointment with not being able to accomplish my original agenda.

My cell phone rang. It was my wife, Diane. With all the guests that had now arrived at the diner, it was loud, so I told Gene and Ray that I'd take the call outside. In the parking lot, a large crow picked aggressively at something on the asphalt. I listened as Diane shared news from home that would change our whole weekend.

○ ○ ○

American writer, journalist and comic strip artist Allen Saunders is quoted as saying, "Life is what happens to you while you're making other plans." Others have said something similar.

Although I know this is often true, I want to control my plans, and life, but sometimes that's like trying to hold water in cupped hands. Still, I would try to save this desert wonderland trip for these guys. I didn't tell them about the nature of my phone call.

As per the agenda, we drove up to the Island in the Sky District in Canyonlands National Park. There is much to see here that doesn't require hiking, climbing or peering over the edge of 1,000 ft. cliffs—well, there are actually several of those. I just didn't mention that small detail, hoping to surprise them once we arrived.

Our first stop was Mesa Arch, a much photographed pothole arch right at the mesa's rim, framing a scenic canyon vista. Mesa Arch spans 50 feet across the top of a 500 ft. vertical drop. The guys walked the easy quarter-mile, well-groomed trail to the arch. A bonus with this arch is that, for the more adventurous, one can actually walk across its narrow top. The two of them would have nothing to do with that. In fact, Gene asked me to get down, and backed away as if somehow I was going to force him to join me. Granted, it would have made a great picture to see them on top, except for the look of terror on their faces.

Our next destination was Grand View Point at the end of the mesa. This vista view overlook—with no guardrail at the edge—provides a seemingly never-ending panorama of how the Colorado River carved the canyons 1,000 feet below us. In my mind, the chances of falling over the cliff to one's brutal, crushing death seemed rather remote. So the gasps of Gene and Ray when I jumped from a rock outcropping across the void and back to the rim seemed a little unwarranted.

A two-mile round trip trail winds along the edge until you run out of mesa. This total distance would be more than the guys' poor feet could tolerate, but they did shamble a bit on the trail until we found a nice spot far from the rim, an area surrounded by whimsical sandstone rock formations. According to plan, this is where we would spilt up, reflect on this fantastical landscape, and start to write out our stories from our notes at breakfast, old school, Ernest Hemingway-style, no laptops.

I found a semi-shady location under a scraggy mesquite tree, the weathered branches giving some relief from the mid-day sun. I sat and grabbed a bag of trail granola from my daypack. My view of the limitless canyons and spire rock formations, with the still snow-capped La Sal Mountains in the background, was indeed inspiring. Something caught my attention by my boot. I dug at it with a stick, and out came an old, rusty engine spark plug. What was that doing out here? Perhaps it was just the spark I needed to ignite the creativity to drive my storytelling from the diner exercise!

But, I couldn't get started, couldn't concentrate, couldn't even reference my notes from breakfast. All I could think about was my phone conversation with Diane. My daughter had had emergency medical surgery early that morning and was in the hospital. Diane had assured me that Sarah's condition, which could have been life threatening, was serious, but that she was stable, improving, and being closely monitored. All of my planning meant nothing to me now.

I had insisted on the phone that I return home immediately, but Diane was adamant that I finish the Moab weekend, knowing how important the time was to me, and what the experience meant to the guys. We had all made a commitment to this outing, and had looked forward to it for months. Diane said that Sarah's medical crisis was under control, and that there really was nothing I could do there. I felt I needed to return to the family, but I didn't want to disappoint Gene and Ray by cutting our time short.

Someone has said, "You can't count on everything going right. But you can count on your friends to be there for you when things go wrong." When I told the guys what had happened, of course, they understood. In fact, they both stated steadfastly that we go directly back to the lodge, pack our bags, and head home right away. And they were dismayed that I hadn't said anything sooner. I suggested that I could call home when we had cell reception again, get an update, and then discuss revised plans.

The guys were so supportive—really there for my family and me. If they were disappointed about having to cut short our trip, they never showed it. Perhaps the hair-raising heights and excruciating foot pain had lost their appeal. Or maybe family matters were far more important to them, and they were insistent that I do what I needed to do, regardless of all the original plans.

News from the home front was good enough for me to suggest a compromise. Sarah would be released from the hospital the next morning. I was now certain I needed to be home, but I felt from the update that we could depart the next morning, and not have to drive home late that night. I *proposed*—didn't plan—that we shorten our stay by one day, but try to catch some featured sights in Arches National Park early the next morning on our way out. The guys agreed—change of plans approved.

Postscript: Our little writers' group, our literary troupe of Three Amigos, returned to Moab the next year. Gene and Ray's feet had mostly healed up and we trekked miles around the remote Needles District of Canyonlands.

Gene and I even hiked way back toward Morning Glory Arch through Negro Bill Canyon. (Ray's heel was flaring up again after the other hikes, so he stayed at the car. The trail was not wheelchair accessible, or I might have considered that for him.) Okay, P.C. folks: Look, I didn't name Negro Bill Canyon—that's what it's officially called on the signs and maps. Apparently, Bill liked the moniker, and no attempts through the years to change the name have been successful. Its historical accuracy has stayed intact.

No one at home got sick. We didn't have to come back to civilization early. We enjoyed the great desert outdoors, critiqued each other's work, and encouraged each other to keep pressing on with this pleasure/pain writing thing.

And, this trip, I was much more relaxed and did not over plan.

I did get around to writing my diner story. If you'd like to read it, here it is below. If not—oh, come on, you want to—skip to the next chapter.

The Next Chapter

Where am I *now*?

I was slow to look around. My head still spun from this latest *tripudiō*. Yeah, the Latin word was right: *a leap*. Wow, I know some Latin? Well, this time, I guess.

"Good morning!" I was greeted way too cheerfully, and by a waitress with a smile impossibly wide for me to accept in my fog. "Take a seat anywhere you'd like." I guess I had just walked in. Don't remember.

A retro-theme diner. Simple, with tacky, this-is-as-much-as-we-could-do-with-our-small-budget 1950s-ish décor. I squinted my eyes as I glanced out the windows to the street. Small town Main Street? The few cars in motion, glinting the early morning light, were not 1950s vintage.

"Thank you," I said, refocusing my attention on the greeter, an older woman with flyaway, grey-blond hair that looked like it had its own internal Tesla Coil. She handed me a stained menu and I shambled down one of two long aisles of mostly empty booths, wondering where I *would* like to sit. Did I care?

I sunk down into the red vinyl seat, next to a window, avoiding two ripped spots in the fabric. What was going on?

Looking down at the menu, I read Moab Diner, "Best Green Chili in Utah." Moab! Had I ever been to Moab? Do I even know where Moab is? Well, in Utah. I felt dizzy and a little ill. Either as a result of the lingering haze from the leap, or the thought of green chili this early in the morning, even if it was the best in Utah.

A semi-truck air-braked on Main Street, slowing to a stoplight. I hadn't at first noticed the red rock cliffs just outside of town. They rose from the desert floor like giant sentinel walls, dwarfing everything below.

A country singer's raspy voice floated from the ceiling speakers in the same way the cooking smells from the kitchen wafted through the diner.

I'm so far from home—home is just a memory...

I guess the diner brand management wasn't too concerned about keeping the authenticity and continuity of the 50s experience. No Elvis or Patty Page? Country Man sang on.

Wandering like before,
What is to be, will be...

I took inventory. Nothing hurt. No apparent injuries, no broken bones, or bruises or scrapes. Not like the last time. And I didn't walk with a limp.

I looked at my clothes: worn jeans, a sports cap, a windbreaker, a down vest. Not much different from the few other early morning patrons. Had I arrived here in my frontier clothes, I probably would not have stood out anyway. Now, if I'd been plopped down here in a blue New York beat cop uniform or a Mars landing spacesuit...that would have gotten some looks! But that's another story.

"Coffee, Hun?" another waitress asked, interrupting my thoughts. She was a large, leathery-faced woman, with eyes that looked in two different directions at the same time. I imagined that if she had a nametag, it probably would have read, Bertha. I reached into my front pocket and pulled out a wad of cash. Bertha may have wondered whether I had robbed a bank, but no doubt hoped I was a big tipper.

"Ah...yes, please." She had a chipped cup in one hand and full pot in the other.

"Careful, it's hot. I'll be back in a few, Dear. After you've had a chance to look at the menu. We've got the best green chili in Utah!" My stomach did a little Irish jig.

Opening the menu, I felt my face, my facial hair. A bushy moustache and matching goatee—that was new! About a three-day growth of whiskers carpeted the rest.

I tried to look at myself in the reflection of a scratched spoon. I pulled off my cap and rubbed my *bald* head. I thought I had thick, black, wavy hair! What was left at the sides looked light brown. My face was sunburned, but otherwise I mostly looked like myself...whoever that was this time.

More breakfast guests began to pour into the brightly lit restaurant. A somber Native American family of six took a larger booth across from me. I wondered why the kids weren't in school.

Bertha returned, ready to refill my still-full cup. "Have you decided yet, Sweety?" We were becoming quite familiar by now with her use of affectionate nicknames. I had a few for her too, but I controlled myself, trying not to stare at the little moustache she had growing. And I didn't know which eye to look at.

"Not just yet, but could you please tell me what day it is today?"

"Well, Saturday, of course! You can always tell that by the number of tourists, and the local families with kids comin' in. They flash flood into here for the best breakfast in town, with the best green chili!"

"What I mean is...the date."

Bertha looked as confused as I felt. "March...the 5th," she answered tentatively, almost in the form of a question, for overstating the obvious.

I hated to continue the inquiry. "And...what...year?"

She looked around as if she might have to call for some muscle from the kitchen to have this lunatic escorted out.

"2011," she spoke more softly, as if not wanting to embarrass me. The color must have left my face. "Are you feeling alright, Honey? Oh...you are just having a little fun with me, right?" She laughed loudly, followed with a snort, then hit me on the shoulder with her order pad.

I smiled a painful, thin smile. "Sorry, I've been...*traveling*. A bit tired, I guess. I'll have two eggs, scrambled dry, and wheat toast...please."

"Not a problem, Sugar. I'll have that right up! Green chili on those eggs?"

"No...thanks."

"Top you off?" She raised the steaming pot.

"I'm fine," I lied. I sank deeper into the bench seat. Moab. 2011. I couldn't believe it.

Every truck stop and restaurant's the same,
No one knows my name,
But all eyes look my way
Not known' I'm just tryin' to survive the cold, cold day...

I felt a shiver. I was last written into a story that was set in the fall of 1828—a younger man, attending an eastern academy. I remember. Massive brick pillars stood on each side of a double lane, old maples...a young love...

I sipped my black coffee. Gads, the brew was still as hot as Hades.

And before that I was a character that stopped for a visit at a small town saloon in the Rockies. Colorado, 2003. Somewhere. I don't remember too much about that. Many good conversations at the tavern...but, clearly, I needed more backstory.

The road is a cruel place then
And yet here I am again
Mile upon mile upon mile
And does this chapter end with a smile?

"Here ya go, Dearest." Bertha clinked the dish on the pink Formica tabletop. "Anything else I can do ya for?" She added a wink with her laugh and snort.

"This is great." I looked down at the plate, rather than allowing my eyes to gravitate to her moustache.

"Holler at me, if you change your mind about a side of that green chili."

I nodded without looking up. I just couldn't.

The food was good—even without the chili. Warming up, I stood to pull off my vest jacket. That's when I saw them, staring at me, all three of them. I froze. They looked away, pretending not to be interested in me.

I knew who they were...and the power they had. We'd met many times before. Well, maybe had *encounters* was a better term. They'd know the right word—they were the ones with the pens and the notebooks and the imaginations and the keyboards. The ones with the whole arsenal of words.

I sat back down. Maybe they hadn't seen me after all. Ridiculous. One of them had written me into this scene: Lost-looking, early morning customer at a diner in Moab. Sports cap. Goatee. Had he just choreographed me to stand to remove my jacket?

I couldn't help it; I had to glance over to their table again. Maybe I could learn something about why I was here. What my story was.

The tall man with the thinning hair began to take some discreet digital photos around the diner interior, looking all the part of a tourist, but I knew better. Those images will be used later for inspiration, just like at the mountain village saloon in Colorado. He squinted his eyes, looking around the room with a balanced amount of cynicism and affection for his fellow diners. He had a keen eye for capturing a moment, but more than that, he could find the meaning of life in every small detail, turning our gaze and hearts upward to something greater than ourselves.

The shorter man with the grey beard had a kind face, knowing, with even kinder eyes, full of whimsy and wonder, looking out through round glasses, into other worlds. He could write of pain that could only be spoken of in a whisper, a hush. Damage that could be bandaged in tender love, healed, but scarred for remembrance, for purpose. I had often wished that it were he who was writing my story more often.

It was the redheaded one that I worried about. He continued to glace my way, looking back down to a binder, taking rapid notes. He was the wild card. Would I be treated with charity, shown grace, or would my pitiful life of self-destruction be used as education for others? He played with his graying weeklong whiskers like a modern-day Faust, trying to gain as much knowledge of me as possible.

Who else in the diner was Red responsible for? What other stories had he written here? Was that fellow sitting by himself over there—the one with the cowboy hat and the Polygamy Pale

Ale t-shirt—a demon-possessed serial killer? Two booths down—that unhappy looking couple—were they both planning for the *accidental* demise of the other for their freedom and selfishness? Was that hairy guy in the corner, with the double rare steak and eggs, really a werewolf, biding his time between full moons? The torn clothes might be a giveaway.

Only Red would know, I guess. I had enough to think about with my own life…or current lack there of. It *was* him this time, I just knew it.

They were gods—with a small g. They had control. The keyboard now mightier than the sword. With imagination and a roll-up-yer-sleeves work ethic in front of an impersonal glowing monitor, they could change lives, if not worlds…the ones *they* had created.

I had considered approaching one or the other of them in the past. You know, offering to buy a beer, and sit down and chat for a while. What better way to get to know me! But I don't know what the rules are. And if they didn't care for that, or were threatened in some way, maybe they'd just delete me. One push of a button. In this story, would Red have me carelessly walk across the street, gazing up, mesmerized by the surrounding sandstone cliffs…and get hit by a semi-truck?

How would I be treated this time? What *is* my story? I guess I'll just have to wait. Life's nothing if not an adventure anyway, right? Who of us really knows what's in store for tomorrow?

I do know I'm a person. Real. Human. Not just a sketch. Not just a background character in a play. More than just words on paper. I've got deep feelings, emotions. I hurt. I long. I hope. I desire that someone cares for me, that I make a difference. That I *was*.

I'll pay Bertha for the meal with cash and a tender smile, looking right into one of her eyes (and past the moustache) and leave a generous tip. She also has a story. Who knows how that might be returned to me? Heck, I might leave the whole wad I found in my pocket. I have no idea where it came from, or what I need it for anyway. I guess that will be written in later.

I stood and put on my vest. Where was I going? Well, that's half the fun, isn't it? Odd, I felt at peace, even with the not knowing. Maybe I was written to be a man of faith. Maybe that's what I *become*, in this story or another. I hope it's that, and not a werewolf or serial killer.

I gave a tip of my cap to Red. He returned a pen salute, and then looked down, continuing to write his notes. My story. Maybe that was a good thing. I'll see these guys again, or they'll see me. I just hope Red doesn't get writer's block—Chapter 111 Word Bankruptcy, or something—that would really stall things.

I stepped out of the diner. The sun had not yet melted the chill off the morning. I cinched up my jacket vest and pulled the collar close to my neck. A large black crow poked at something flat and hard in the parking lot.

The music from the diner's interior also played from speakers on the outside of the building. Whether time had stood still, or their playlist repeated in a loop, Country Man sang on...

I'm on my way, hurrying to somewhere
The next chapter
I'm on my way
To the next chapter.

Fatty McButterbutt vs. the Thunderstorm

Sawtooth Ridge, Mount Evans
to Mount Bierstadt, and Back Again

"There is no such thing as bad weather, only different kinds of good weather."

— John Ruskin, 1819-1900 —

Given John Ruskin's cheery and charitable view of weather, it's clear he had never hiked at high altitude in the Rockies. An English writer and art critic, Mr. Ruskin had certainly seen his share of damp London fog and bitter Dickens-like winters of despair. It seems that with his optimism toward life in England, he might have also concluded, "There is no such thing as bad teeth, only different kinds of teeth."

Our little troop of intrepid climbers—my brother-in-law, Kevin, my son-in-law, Joe, my granddaughter, Maren, and her friend, Keira—started our mid-July day with such enthusiasm. What would be so tough about this? I had climbed Mt. Bierstadt six times (twice in winter), summited Mt. Evans two times, and had been across the legendary Sawtooth Ridge three times. Sure, it would involve climbing two 14ers in one day, and crossing a challenging, but fun, traverse, but how bad could it be, really? We planned to start from the top of Evans (there is a paved road nearly to the summit), follow a descending contour to the ridge, cross the Sawtooth, ascend Mt. Bierstadt, and return the same way. Piece of cake.

This was our first fourteener climb of the season. I had done some local, moderate trail hiking, but nothing very long, and not in the high country. And, okay, I'll admit, I was still carrying some compounded winter weight, going all the way back to gorging on Christmas cookies months before. But for Joe to be calling me "Fatty McButterbutt" was nothing short of cruel.

Now, for my loving son-in-law to unkindly label me was a little like the pot calling the kettle black. I refuse to return evil for evil, but let's just generously say that Joe was not in his prime training-for-Olympic-wrestling days himself. To his point, it is very important, especially for climbing 14ers, to be able to actually *see* your feet below you as you negotiate steps through treacherous terrain. I could stand to lose a few pounds around the mid section for safety, and stamina.

The drive up the mountain gave us some cause for concern, as the clouds were already building rapidly—unusual for the Rockies this early in the morning. We were confident we would drive above the weather system, and we did. By the time we reached the Mt. Goliath Natural Area, home to scraggly 1,500-year-old bristlecone pines (youngsters by bristlecone standards), we were looking down on cloud-carpeted valleys.

At the parking area on the top of Evans (elevation 14,264 ft.), we were greeted by a curious Rocky Mountain Bighorn Sheep, out for an alpine climb as well, We stretched, downed some more water, put on gloves and knit hats, threw on our well-stocked packs (my waist strap let out some), grabbed our hiking sticks and started out over fresh snow on the trail—yes, fresh snow from the night before, in July. This would be Keira's first 14er experience, and the 6th and 7th for Maren.

○ ○ ○

Our family has always enjoyed the great outdoors, and when Maren came on the scene, she just joined the crowd in motion. Whether jiggling and giggling in her Daddy's child backpack as we trudged up the rocky trail steps to Hanging Lake by Glenwood Springs, Colorado, or fishing with Grandpa for cutthroat trout in a gurgling mountain creek, she didn't just go along compliantly, she attacked the wilderness with infectious enthusiasm. Like her mother, Sarah, when she was young, Maren couldn't pass a boulder without climbing to the top or a tree branch without hanging off it, upside down. Of course, these were always great photo ops for Mom.

We still laugh at the time we were fishing Four-Mile Creek in Colorado with 3-year-old Maren. Of course, she wanted to try it. Her casting needed work, as her line frequently found its way into brush around her, eventually ripping the worm off the hook. We were using large night crawlers that had to be "pinched" in half to fit the hook and to lure these smaller trout. We asked Maren if she wanted to rip the worms in two, and she did so several times with great gusto! That is until she burst into tears realizing these were actual living, bleeding, gut-spilling worms, and not like her Gummi Worms at home. Maren was as compassionate about her wilderness experience as she was passionate.

Now I'm not *fishing* for compliments here (sorry), but I should explain why I'm back on 14ers again, after having completed them all in eight years before turning 50. Why I'm carrying my big bottom up to the top of these beasts again. It's Maren. Following her first summit with me, and her daddy, Joe, she was hooked.

Some time ago, on our way up Maren's starter 14er, Mt. Sherman, we paused at a short ridge to catch our breath and enjoy the panoramic views while I identified some of the other peaks in the region. I told Maren that as I get older (and fatter), I might not be able to do the toughest ones with her. She and her dad might have to do those as I cheer them on from below, so to speak.

"But, Papa," she said, "who will help us to the top? Who will show us the way? We need you." I felt a lump in my throat—maybe just half of a pinched worm.

She continued, "Who will point out the other 14ers, on another range? Who will show us Mt. Elbert? The five peaks of Mt. Massive? You have to keep doing this!"

Now I'm the one on a hook, and she's reeling me in! So, I'm on my second round, and will climb these mountains, guiding and showing the way, God willing, as long as I can (and, hopefully, lighter on my feet).

Maren reflecting her enthusiasm for 14ers (and Grandpa in her stylish sunglasses).

The five of us descended the Evans summit, amazed, as we looked 1,000 feet down at Abyss Lake and across a huge bowl separating Evans and Bierstadt except for the ominous Sawtooth Ridge on the north end. The only other climbers we encountered had come the other way from Bierstadt and shared the good news that there was no snow on the Sawtooth. We crossed a vast, open, high-elevation meadow punctuated with lichen-covered boulders, and surprisingly little trail evidence. We could now clearly see the difficulties ahead—a seemingly impossible trail along a thin, jagged ridge, marked only by a few cairns. I'd been here before, yet still found the view of the route jaw dropping. We carefully negotiated the zigzag, up and down knife edge, rounded or topped rocks splintered off the cliffs, helping each other by best route finding or holding sticks so that others could use both hands for scrambling.

When we crossed over the ridge through a crux point to the other side, our view opened up the summit climb to Mt. Bierstadt.

We knew where we had to go—up—but no clear trail was apparent through a steep boulder field. We spread out, and shouted back and forth, hoping one would find strong trail clues. As it turned out, there were probably hundreds of "trails" to the top.

We did have one little scare. Joe reached up once for stability, and to his surprise, the large rock above his head that he was holding came loose and he nearly fell backwards. (I maintain he just doesn't know his own strength.) He had the athleticism and wherewithal to throw his head forward, and at the same time toss the rock over and behind him. Now, Joe is kind of hardheaded, but if he hadn't done this some-type-of-wrestling move, he'd be, at the very least, a few inches shorter today.

The weather was still holding for us on the Bierstadt Summit, but clouds were charging in from all directions. Not much time to enjoy the views, and we still were only half done—we had to return the way we came. We did not want to cross the dreaded Sawtooth during a typical Colorado afternoon thunderstorm. We quickly ate our snack lunch, signed the register sheet, took the congratulatory summit "high-five" and hugs photos, and headed back down the steep slope towards the ridge. Picking up the trail for the descent was as hard and time-consuming as it was going up.

Back to the crux opening and through to the other side of the ridge we looked back at Bierstadt to see the top now shrouded in mean clouds. Thick, wraith weather fronts now began rushing the peaks all around us. The clouds spilled over ridges and snaked their way down to and up valleys with ill intent. It was mesmerizing. Distant thunder moved closer. We had to get off the mountain, and now!

We were moving quickly, determinedly, but carefully. At a saddle, we paused to catch our breath. I didn't realize just how much I was spent. The others seemed to be doing okay, but I hit a wall and had to sit down. Not enough pre-season practice hikes, underestimating (short memory!) the difficulty of this climb, and yes, carrying too much buttery body weight. Kevin saw I was struggling and offered me a high-energy GU , which I reluctantly squeezed down my throat.

A huge thunderclap exploded over our heads, shaking the ground. Time to go! Whether pushed by adrenaline or GU power, I was on the move again with the others. The Sawtooth and the storm were not going to beat me!

We scrambled up a very steep, narrow cliff edge and spilled out into the exposed open area between the two peaks, and the clouds overtook us. The wet fog was so thick we couldn't see 10 yards ahead of us. Any trail was weak here anyway, and in this pea soup we could make out no cairns for direction. We all stayed close together. Thunder roiled all around us, but fortunately we'd seen no close lightning.

The world closed in around us with zero visibility, our own close forms just dark, blurry silhouettes to each other. Orienting ourselves was impossible. We knew generally the direction we had to go and pulled out our compasses to help confirm; our damp maps were useless. We couldn't even see Mt. Evans where we were supposed to be heading, and there was the danger that we'd get too near a cliffy area close to the return trail.

The temperature dropped dramatically; our thermometers now read 37 degrees. Out came the extra clothing, gloves and balaclavas or knit caps. Grapple snow (small hail or sleet) began to pelt us from somewhere inside the cloud, and fell hard enough to start to cover the ground. We wandered, eyes squinting and searching for something familiar, some landmark, some hint of a trail. There! Cairns ... and a well-beaten path. We found it. This had to be our trail!

Up ... up ... up. This was a strong trail. But something was wrong. We were supposed to gently contour up, back along the side of Evans, to the parking lot. This just didn't feel right. Too steep. We were disoriented in the fog, which now spit freezing rain straight into our faces, but we knew this couldn't be the right route. Still, we continued on a bit further to try to glean some clue as to our whereabouts.

We reached a peak, but discovered this wasn't our destination! We were on the top of an entirely different mountain. We had taken a wrong turn somewhere, and wound up ... here. Kevin pulled out his GPS, and confirmed our suspicion: we had summited Mount Spaulding. This was a smaller, adjoining peak, on the way to Evans, and not where we wanted to be. When we finally got out today, we will have climbed three peaks! This was deflating, but we had to try to keep our spirits as high as our elevation, retrace our path, and press forward to find our route out. What else could happen to us?

Halfway back down Mt. Spaulding, it began to rain. It came on us fast, and hard. With the temperature dropping, to be soaking wet could bring a quick onset of hypothermia. We hurriedly got our rain ponchos out of our packs, but the torrent was so heavy, and hitting us sideways, that staying dry was a challenge. New-formed rivulets soon became full-on streams everywhere. Back down to the alpine meadows, we sloshed through accumulating water runoff that had nowhere to go.

Close thunder boomed around us again, as if the storm were taunting us for our poor judgment. This was a bad situation—one to be strictly avoided by climbers—and one that was about to get worse. We had talked with the girls on our way up in the car about extreme weather conditions on mountains, and what were some possibilities we might expect. Of course, we never imagined we'd be hit with everything in one day!

Maren and Keira got a little bit ahead of the group, but then came running back with panicked looks on their faces. We were shocked to see the hair on their heads standing straight up! The air around us was super-charged with static electricity. We were now all walking lightning rods in this very exposed area.

Lightning lit up the fog, followed by another crash right above us. I yelled instructions for us to spread out while we continued to where Mt. Evans should be. We kept each other in sight, but created distance between us so that if the worst happened, we wouldn't—in a microsecond— automatically be lit-up conductors to the next person. I sent a little prayer heavenward, through the cloud cover, that we'd find the correct trail soon.

A new round of hail beat down on us. Apparently, we hadn't been punished enough yet. We took cover, bunched together under a short overhang by a cluster of large rocks. Our gloves were soaked through, water trickled down our backs, finding its way into the parkas at the neck, and our boots and hiking pants had become one with the marshland around us.

As fast as it came upon us the fog cleared, allowing us to finally see Mt. Evans. We set off again, and soon picked up the cairns and trail that would take us back to the parking lot. We trudged upward over slippery rocks and a hail-covered path. Driving rain and sleet stung our faces.

Kevin and Keira moved ahead of the three of us. We hoped we'd find them at the top, waiting in a warmed car for us. I was totally exhausted, but had to dig even deeper for the strength to continue, as Maren and Joe seemed to be struggling even more. It had been a long, hard day, but I don't think the GU they had ingested sat well with them. There was a green tint to their wet faces.

Step by step, yard by yard, turn by turn, I encouraged them up the trail. Cold, soaked, dog-tired, we had to get out of there. One foot after the other, with too many rest stops, we slowly worked our way to the top. What a welcome sight to come around a bend and see the parking lot with Kevin and the car! Fatty McButterbutt, and his little posse of double-fatigued, sponge-soaked, triple-mountain climbers, had beaten the daunting Sawtooth Ridge, and survived everything the thunderstorm could throw at us.

○ ○ ○

Postscript: We made it over the Sawtooth Ridge connecting Bierstadt and Evans and off the mountain. But not everyone has. A little over a week after our climb, 32-year-old Clinton McHugh died in a fall while hiking the ridge-top trail. He had just moved from Chicago and was enjoying Colorado.

McHugh had called his wife around noon from the summit of Mt. Bierstadt. He then climbed the Sawtooth with a group of people taking the ridge route to Mt. Evans. For some reason, McHugh turned back, alone, and fell some 250 feet to his death.

It was reported that severe weather moving through the area that afternoon might have played a role in his accident.

Twisted Logic

Mount Herman, Pike National Forest, CO

"Well!" thought Alice to herself. "After such a fall as this, I shall think nothing of tumbling down stairs!"

— *Alice's Adventures in Wonderland*, by Lewis Carroll —

I hadn't broken a bone since I was just a year old. One evening I had scrambled up a chair (apparently I was into adventure climbing at a very young age), promptly did an endo over the side, and broke my arm. Of course, regarding my rappelling with no rope, before I could even walk, I have no recollection of this La-Z-Boy infant mountaineering accident. My mother tells me I cried like a baby.

Mom still has the tiny cast in a memory box somewhere, signed with scribbles by my Sierra Madre, California, neighborhood toddler friends, and splattered with mystery Gerber food stains. Accompanying it are faded get-well cards from extended family members. This all sounds wonderfully sentimental, but Mom didn't tell me until years later that because there was no obvious head trauma or bruising about the face and neck, she assumed I was fine and just put me to bed. It wasn't until the next morning, as I was still complaining of the pain (okay, in the only way I knew how), that she took me to the doctor's office. How I must have suffered terribly, all night, alone in my crib, in the dark.

○ ○ ○

Fast forward to Colorado, October 2010. It was a beautiful, sunny, unseasonably warm Fall Sunday. I had decided to take my little dog, Lance, on a hike and have "church" on the mountain not far from our home. Sir Lancelot is a gentle, friendly, curly-haired—don't laugh now—black cockapoo. He's more cocker spaniel-like, with long legs, plenty of enthusiasm, and loves to explore the wilderness with me. I know he doesn't sound like a very manly mountain dog, but, please don't tell him that. He has no idea he is part poodle.

Mt. Herman is in the Pike National Forest on the Rampart Range, the eastern Front Range between Denver and Colorado Springs. The peak climbs only to 8,947 feet (not too impressive since the trailhead starts around 7,200 feet), but on a clear day views from the top include "America's Mountain," Pikes Peak, to the south and Longs Peak to the north, as well as the Colorado Springs and Denver skylines. The easiest, conventional route up is a moderate Class 1 trail that passes scenic, aspen-lined creeks and gently winds up boulder-strewn canyons. Lance and I took another route.

I had been on this alternate trail several times, especially when my kids were young. We enjoyed the climb up above a waterfall to an outcropping called Inspiration Point, where we could look down on the charming, Lilliputian-like town of Palmer Lake. But I had never summited Mt. Herman from this side before. Lance seemed uninterested in the views, so we pressed onward and upward through a long, steep gravel ascent to a ridge. It's along this ridge trail that the kids and I coined the name "The Rock Garden" for an aspen grove section spotted with huge, house-sized boulders that are fun for climbing and exploring around.

Past the stone garden playground Lance and I stopped and sat for a drink and snacks I had brought in my fanny pack. We needed fuel and hydration before the next uphill part of the trail through the pine woods I knew to be particularly narrow, steep and rocky—the final stretch that I had only observed from a distance. Shared cool water, beef jerky and cut pieces of apple invigorated us for the push to the top. Lance seemed to be a little miffed that the beef jerky was not divided out evenly, but, hey, at eight bucks a bag, I'm sorry, Mister. Get a job.

T. Duren Jones

The ascent was broken and loose, with uneven natural rock steps and decomposed granite marbles that made going slow. Hard to even call it a trail. I remember thinking at the time that this was going to be tough coming down on our way back. I was glad for the forecast of clear skies. This would have been really nasty if wet.

We broke out of the trees and did summit to a glorious, warm, cloudless day. No light breeze even stirred the thin alpine blades of grass. I had a family luncheon that I had to get back for, but I still had some time to enjoy the views. I understand that on a clear day, the average person at 10,000 feet can see just over 120 miles. It felt to me that I could see thousands of miles in every direction.

It is times like these, sitting alone on the top of a mountain, that I have been so grateful for my faculties, my physical health, my eyesight, my ability to climb peaks, and for the privilege of living in this beautiful region of the country. These are gifts. Thank God that I take none of it for granted. Lance, on the other hand, was just interested in marking his territory, chasing butterflies and sniffing the fanny pack for any more beef jerky. He's so shallow. After a few more minutes of reflection, it was time for us to start down.

The first steep part of the trail was difficult to descend, as expected. I wished I had four legs like my buddy who was leading. It was slow going, but good to be cautious. If I went down hard here, I was alone, no cell service, no help or rescue.

At a particularly sharp-sloping section, with exposed tree roots intersecting the gravel trail, I heard a group of hikers talking in the distance, and barking dogs, the noise from the forest nearing us. Everything from this point happened so fast it is hard to state clearly what exactly transpired. But it changed my life for months to come.

Two large dogs, off leash, rounded a switchback and were running up the trail straight towards us. I had no idea what their intent was. Their masters were yelling for their return, but the commands were ignored. Were they just friendly, excited, curious about meeting Lance, wanting a beef jerky snack? Or did they have a hostile agenda, to help themselves to a bite of cockapoo? I couldn't wait to see. I scooped the little fella up into my arms.

At this point I didn't really know what I was thinking. Just reacting, I guess. Protect Lance. See what these other dogs had in mind. Protect myself. Get down off this precarious section of the trail to solid footing (better defensive posture?). Move forward to close the gap with the irresponsible dog owners to see what their plan was for these disobedient pooches. All of the above?

The masters continued to call back their runaways, to no avail. The dogs kept charging. I held Lance higher and closer to my chest. Some of my thought process seemed to make sense at the time. The rush decisions had a certain foggy logic to them. But my choices produced classic hiker mistakes that cost me.

In having Lance up around my face, I could not see where to plant my feet. I looked ahead on the trail and did not pay enough attention to the ground beneath me. I was off balance. I was shaken and distracted by the rapidly approaching Hounds of Hell. Because I was holding Lance, I wasn't able to use my hiking stick for another point of stability. Instead of getting my bearings, I decided to move forward to get off this steep incline.

My right foot slipped on gravel. My ankle slid down into a hole at an odd angle. My leg twisted. I went down hard on my rear still holding on to Lance. Severe pain shot through me.

Immediately, I had two *odd* thoughts:

1) "You've just broken your leg," I told myself. Odd, because I had no memory of the one-year-old recliner incident and its associated pain (and subsequent cover-up by Mom), so thereby no point of reference.
2) "Why am I talking to myself in the 2nd person?" (This turned out to be something I did a lot over the course of the next few hours.)

But this couldn't be a break. Just a turned ankle. A bad sprain, that's all.

I sat for a few moments, evaluating, defenseless against the slobbering canines approaching. It turned out that they weren't Satan's minions after all, just exuberant, inquisitive, puppy-like dogs. They licked my face, and sniffed Lance's backside (something that thankfully separates us from the animal world). Then they were off, running up the trail, still ignoring the hiker-master calls.

The group had arrived in time to see the whole incident, were very apologetic, and asked if there was anything they could do. I stood, shambled a few paces, thanked them, and then, embarrassed, mumbled something silly about an old football injury and that I would just sit and rest for a few minutes. More of their apologies followed. Soon, they were off chasing their canines and I never saw them again.

Surely, I had just twisted my ankle. I'd be okay in a few minutes.

The few minutes passed, and I wasn't any better. But I had to get out of there. No one was carrying me out. No cell connection to call for assistance. And I couldn't send Lance, like a TV Lassie, back to the ranch to get help. "You can do this, you can do this" I told myself reassuringly.

I took a couple of Tylenol, gulped down half a Nalgene bottle of water, cinched up my bootlaces tightly, and started out. I've played a lot of sports and had a few injuries over the years, but I had never felt pain like this. To call my slow, stutter-walk a hobble would have been generous. I could put no weight on the leg at all without shooting pain nearly immobilizing me. I leaned on my hiking stick, one excruciating step after another. Nothing eased the discomfort. I was close to crying like a baby but kept my stoic composure in front of Lance. No reason to promote widespread panic.

I tried different types of steps, thinking I could find one style of walking that worked better than another. Nothing helped. Minutes literally turned to hours as I painfully plodded on. I had to keep going since it was over a two-mile trek back to the car.

Lance appeared to sense something was wrong. He usually ran up the trails ahead of me, alpha dog style, but now held back behind me to make sure I would make it. Going was slow. The bad news was that we were already late for lunch, and now we risked missing dinner. One skipped meal I could accept; two was unthinkable.

The good news was that we did make it out off the mountain. Sometimes dragging the useless leg; sometimes crawling. I did not have to spend the night, or days, in the wilderness. I did not have to eat my little buddy to stay alive. As loving as he is, he probably would have been willing to give up his life for me. The irony didn't escape me: that I had sacrificed my ankle for Lance's safety, saving his life from mad dogs, only to have to eat him later for survival. (I'm kidding, of course. Really.)

The next morning, I could put no weight on the leg, making the early bathroom run particularly challenging. My wife, Diane, insisted that she take me to the local EmergiCare (with me insisting that it was still just a bad sprain). X-rays revealed a spiral fracture of my fibula. The next nine weeks would include multiple trips to the orthopedic surgeon, a boot cast and crutches, wearing shorts through a cold Colorado winter, and daydreaming about getting back up a mountain again. Physical therapy lasted even longer.

I did (thankfully) fully recover and hike several trails as well as summit four 14ers the following summer. I can tell you that I'm much more careful now on my hikes, watching my step placement closely, and not allowing myself to become overly distracted. An older Lance does more neighborhood walks with me now rather than mountain hiking. No mad dogs off leash have attacked us lately.

Making Lists and Punishing Friends

El Diente Peak, San Miguel Mountains, Colorado

"Life is either a daring adventure or nothing at all."

— Helen Keller —

I am goal-oriented. I like to have a plan, a strategic approach, and guiding measurements for achievement. I like to look back at accomplishments and take a certain pride at the successes. Perhaps this comes somewhat from my career years in publishing and marketing, driven by planning and deadlines.

I like lists, especially checklists with boxes I can tick off to show progress. I make a list of the lists I need to make. I live off of yellow sticky notes, giving reminders, direction and priorities to my day or week. I will often make a rough draft list that I will eventually transfer to another, more final list. And I will sometimes add assignments that I've already completed to an existing list just to be able to check them off (beaming at my own productivity prowess).

So, it should come as no surprise that I had a checklist for climbing all the Colorado Fourteeners. The guidebooks divide the 54 peaks over 14,000 ft. into levels of difficulty—moderate to very difficult. Some books even have a wonderful checklist by category, with nice little boxes, in the back pages. How great is that?

For the most part, I followed the lists, starting with the "easier" ones, and those with the shorter traveling distance from my home on the Eastern Front Range of the Rockies. I progressed to the more difficult ones after gaining more endurance, experience and confidence. I was driven by my self-imposed goal (maybe a dumb one) of finishing all of the 14ers by age 50. It took me 8 years to summit all those monster mountains, and I completed my last one three days before my self-imposed deadline.

Bruce Peppin, my best friend from childhood (who had also moved to Colorado from Southern California), had climbed several 14ers with me. He doesn't have a crazy obsession, like mine, but he loves the outdoors and simply wanted to do stuff with me, and to experience what I enjoyed so much. When climbing with me, he made unbelievable sacrifices for our friendship: enduring sleepless nights camping at trailheads; ascending ridiculously steep, rocky slopes, sometimes off trail; trekking additional blister-producing miles of trails when his "guide" got lost; and forcing himself to push through his fear of heights. But, that's what friends do for each other, I guess. That doesn't explain what I did to the poor guy on El Diente Peak.

Bruce supported my mountaineering passion as he did other areas in my life. Friends since the third grade, we were much closer than most brothers; we were buddies. He and I shared many great memories of our climbs together, and he also wanted to hear the stories of my other summits. Together, we got to experience the "Rocky Mountain Highs" through the struggles to the top, and the joys of the "elevation celebration" at our accomplishments. So I can't justify, then, why I would want to deliberately punish him.

As Bruce knew the importance to me of finishing my 14er list, of course he insisted on being with me for the ceremonial completion: summiting my only remaining peak, the last box to be checked on my laborious, long-awaited goal. I was thrilled. This was especially meaningful because I knew he was aware that this would not be an easy climb, one that would push him to the edge, or beyond, of the limits of his confidence and endurance levels.

Our adventure started with a great dinner the night before (of course) at my favorite brewery restaurant in Telluride. Because of the drive, and of our late arrival, we had decided to "car camp" in the back of my SUV at the trailhead, rather than take the time to tent camp. This would allow us a faster morning departure, and no camp breakdown following a long climbing day. We hoped for a good night's sleep, but I think we were both too excited for that to happen.

Up early, with headlamps on in the dark, we double-checked our pack supplies, put on our gloves, knit caps and lightweight windbreakers, to stave off the early July pre-dawn chill. We started out, choosing to energy snack and hydrate on our way.

I wouldn't put El Diente Peak (14,159 ft.) in the top 10 list of the most difficult Colorado 14er climbs, but it is close, and still very challenging. I had not left it to the end because it is such a tough one, but because of its long driving distance from my home north of Colorado Springs. It is located in the Lizard Head Wilderness in southwestern Colorado. I had actually tried to climb El Diente (Spanish for "The Tooth," describing its shape at the top) one year before, on Labor Day, but was pushed off it by a surprise whiteout blizzard early in the morning.

After not much more than two miles of trail ascent through lush forest and wildflower-speckled alpine meadows, Bruce had a concerned look on his face. We stopped by a dramatic waterfall, still fed by snowmelt. The setting was picture-perfect spectacular, with the backdrop of the roaring fall, and up the valley to the tooth-like top of our peak. Bruce was already perspiring heavily.

"There's something wrong with my drinking tube," he said with some consternation.

"What do you mean?" I asked. The tube that ran back into a reservoir in his pack looked okay to me. We could not afford any problems—we had a lot of hiking ahead of us.

"I can't get anything out of it! Sucking as hard as I can … and nothing!"

"Maybe it's pinched off, kinked, or something," I suggested reassuringly. "Let's take a look."

Bruce stripped off his pack and we followed the tube path back into the cargo area. Things seemed okay.

"Maybe the bladder has a leak in it, and I've lost all my water," he said. We checked the outside of his pack, but it was bone dry.

Tales from the Trails

"Let's look inside," I directed.

He unloaded all his extra clothing, gear and food. We got to the sealed reservoir and pulled it out. It was completely empty! We *had* started this climb with conversation about the importance of proper hydration, but in the first couple of miles, Bruce had completely finished off *all* his water! Not a drop left. Nada. Dry as a desert. Sucking-air empty.

Fortunately, I try to come prepared for any situation, and I had a filtered water bottle. We ran stream water through it and refilled Bruce's Camelbak reservoir. We also packed an extra Nalgene water bottle with snow in a mile or so. We would repeat this again later in the day for this thirsty hiker!

I was surprised to see such a large snowfield on the mountainside, assuming it would have melted by this time. Following our trail directions and map, it looked like our route up this valley took us right through it. We cautiously traversed diagonally across the steep snow pack, digging in our boots with each slow step. If we slipped, we would have slid down into a glacier-deposited pile of angular rocks. The going was unnerving, and the pace time consuming and energy draining as we trail blazed and post-holed, using our hiking sticks for stability.

Past the snowfield, we really began to climb. We had to do a bit of tedious orienteering through several cliff bands, and eventually struggled to a scree slope below the Organ Pipe gendarmes—huge rock pinnacles. This was challenging stuff, and we were more than aware of how careful we had to be.

Working our way across the mountainside below a ridge, we encountered a deep snow-filled couloir that our rocky route had to cross. We stopped to ponder the situation. The surrounding terrain was steep and treacherous, so going up, or down, and around it was not an option. We'd worked too hard to turn back. But would the snow-packed gully hold for us? Even as experienced at mountain climbing as I was, I still had trepidation about this passage. Well, there was only one way to find out. I told Bruce that if I didn't make it ... he should *NOT* try to continue.

At this point, I think I'll let Bruce jump in to continue our story from his own journal:

> "The trek became arduous from 11,500 feet on, where all the vegetation gives way to rocky talus and huge boulders. We could hear where icy water was gushing under the rocks, but couldn't see it. We followed little cairns that marked the direction of the path.
>
> Several times on the way up, I thought about turning around and calling it quits. Nearly eight hours had passed and we still hadn't conquered the peak. Exhaustion was starting to take hold and I knew I had to get to the top, and soon.
>
> I rounded a turn hoping to view the summit. Instead I was dismayed to see that the path narrowed to barely 12 inches wide with a 500 ft. drop off on the right side. For the first time in my hiking experience I felt fear. If I lost my balance I could topple over the edge to my death. This was not a good situation as I was already beat and my legs were spent.
>
> Tim carefully walked across that stretch of narrow rock. He motioned for me to cross over knowing that I could do it. I sat there for a few minutes and asked for help from above.
>
> I then stood up and walked across that rock ledge. I could see the top now. There was only one more obstacle in our way. This time a snow-covered crevasse blocked our path. It was about 15 feet across and at a 45° angle with another drop off at the edge of the snow. All I had to do was push my boots into its steep face and work my way to the other side. However, if the snow gave way under my weight, there would be no way to stop from sliding off where the snow ended to certain death. Tim went first, and then assured me I could make it. Challenged once more to overcome my fear, I breathed another prayer and crossed over.
>
> Finally, I had made it to the top and reveled in the incredible views. It was the hardest climb I had ever

done and it felt great to be at the summit. We shared high-fives and hugs. But, we couldn't stay long due to degrading weather conditions.

I re-crossed those two obstacles on the way down with no further stalling. Fourteen hours after our start, at 8:00 pm, Tim and I made it back to his truck at the trailhead. We packed up our gear and headed home.

Tim had reached a milestone few achieve by summiting all the 14ers in Colorado. It was great to be a part of that accomplishment. I also took with me important life lessons about overcoming fear, the power of friendship, and doggedly pressing ahead to reach a goal."

I'm not sure it was quite as dramatic as Bruce described. But then, I tend to have a short memory about these things. Or, I live in some sort of denial, as I'm ready to get on to the next high-altitude adventure. *That wasn't so bad*, I'll think to myself, on my drive home.

○ ○ ○

The way back seemed no less arduous, with steep declines, marble-like gravel underfoot, and the same boulder and snowfields, in reverse, that had impeded our progress on our way up. When we finally found our way back to flat ground below the waterfall, Bruce dropped to his hands and knees and playfully feigned crawling, so thankful to be back on terra firma, exhausted, but alive. We still had a couple of miles hiking back to the SUV, but the danger of falling 1,000 ft. to an ugly death was behind us.

What kind of a friend would deliberately put himself, or herself, in a place completely outside of his or her comfort zone … for the sake of another? Of course, the question could also be asked, as in my case: Who would make someone else do such a thing? I'm guilty but well-meaning.

Bruce was so glad to be down off of El Diente Peak!

Who, for the sake of the friendship, would allow himself to be tested in extreme conditions? Who would have to push through personal fears and challenges, would conquer the obstacles, and because he or she *wants* to be there to share in the victory, despite the discomfort and pain?

I have such a friend, and I am grateful. Bruce and I shared together the ordeal and the celebration of accomplishment—for me, the triumph of a life goal. I was privileged to have Bruce's support, encouragement, and companionship (on six peaks) on this endeavor.

○ ○ ○

Epilog: I have started my second round of summiting all the 14ers, this time with my granddaughter, Maren. She has her own checklist, with little boxes. I'm so proud.

Conquering Contrast Canyon

Lathrop Canyon, Island in The Sky, Canyonlands, Utah

"'Let the music play on' would be my legacy."

— Lionel Ritchie —

We are all familiar with the often-overused phrase, "everyone's got a story," but it's true. I've lived many stories from my hikes around the West, and have discovered others. And I enjoy sharing them. Sometimes, over and over again. Groucho Marx once said, "If you've heard this story before, don't stop me, because I'd like to hear it again." So, keep reading.

I love to hear other people's stories. I enjoy learning about the chapters in their lives, their journeys, their challenges, the paths they took, and the outcomes. In the long run, the stories of our lives—for better or worse—may outlive us.

Part of my story is that I have had extraordinary opportunities to encounter the beauty and purity of nature by myself, or shared with others. I have taken "the road less traveled" many times and have experienced remarkable times in the wild. I have learned many life lessons from the trials (and lived to tell about them!), and have been able to glean insights from the life stories of others as well.

I have hiked hundreds of miles, on countless wilderness trails, with Diane, Kevin, family and friends. Together, we have seen magnificent scenery time and time again. But we have also discovered interesting episodes from the history of our nation, and from those who went before us who helped define it, for good or for bad. My late-winter hike with Kevin on the Lathrop Trail in Canyonlands National park was no exception.

Tales from the Trails

This was the last of several trails we had hiked that dropped from the Island in the Sky mesa down to the White Rim Road plateau below. We had held off doing this 11-mile round-trip route because of the daunting two-mile plodding meadow trek before even reaching the 1,000 ft. descent off the edge. This winter day, trudging through a foot of fresh snow added to the challenge.

Part of this story was our temptation to turn back because of the difficulty and the unknown. We had not brought our snowshoes—typically they are not needed for high desert hikes—so our pace had been slow and laborious. We did get to laugh because the snow built on our soles making our boots platform shoes. I appreciated the extra four to five inches of height.

We stopped to discuss our options, including whether we should even continue. Our biggest concern was the snow and ice we anticipated encountering on the drop off. We had done many snow hikes in the Moab region, but none down and up such a steep cliff face. We decided to explore a bit further to see the conditions ahead.

It's easy to be so focused on trail finding and foot placement that one may miss what's happening all around. There probably have been times I failed to notice some wonderful scenic views because I was concentrating so hard looking down at a rough path. I guess I really wouldn't know.

Just as we approached the rim, I happened to look over at a snow-covered rock pile and spotted a big horned sheep warily watching us, no doubt amused at our heavy-footed lack of progress. What a rare treat to see a big ram in a natural setting like this! I'm sure I frustrated Kevin by taking so much time shooting so many photos, but I couldn't pass up the opportunity.

We pressed on, and much to our surprise, close to the mesa edge, the snow had melted off on this sunny, eastern side. Had we decided to turn back, we would have missed some great hiking memories. A series of cairns helped us cross past slickrock domes and potholes, and then down a sandy arroyo peppered with piñon and juniper trees.

We followed a narrow bench to a rocky slide area. This portion of the trail was very steep, but made manageable—with careful foot placement—by a long series of tight switchbacks. Leaving the rock pile, the path began to level out near the bottom of Upper Lathrop Canyon, and our route followed a heavily eroded old mining road. It was at this point that we saw the first bright yellow warning sign.

The Future is Bright?

Walking the dirt road gave us a glimpse into the interesting, and tragic, uranium mining boom that took place in Canyonlands in the 1950s. We looked to both sides of the canyon and saw several abandoned mine shafts—at least six of them within a few hundred yards of the old road. Each had been gated by the National Park Service and had posted warnings of the presence of radioactive material inside the mines and in the tailings.

Signs at the mine entrances read "Do Not Enter," along with other warnings against drinking the seasonal creek water below the mine openings, and avoiding any springs in the area, some of them contaminated by snow melt or rain runoff. Seriously? They have to tell us that?

The thought did briefly cross my mind that if I drank some of that radioactive water, maybe I wouldn't need a flashlight in the dark, and I could "Hulk" up for the spring softball league. We are environmentally conscious, but that would give new meaning to being "green." Kevin reminded me of what happened to those radiated giant ants from those corny sci-fi movies from the '50s. We chose to round these areas as widely as possible, and not dip a cup.

The sad story was that these unregulated radioactive mines had their heyday during the "uranium frenzy" of the Cold War era. Whether out of corporate ignorance, negligence, or knowing intent, this chapter in our nation's history left a path of illness and death, still impacting families decades later. It's hard to believe that uranium was once added to toothpaste as a whitener, was put in children's sand boxes, included in florescent glass pitchers, and was used as face paint for that fun "glow-in-the-dark" party trick.

During the Second World War, Navajo miners were hired to excavate uranium ore from which "yellow cake" would be extracted for the first atomic bombs. Some reports state that the U. S. government was very aware of the hazards, but did not warn the miners. Some miners took the tailings home—most of them eventually died of cancer.

In the 1950's, uranium was mined for hand-painted, luminescent clock faces and hands. Young women in factories used to apply uranium-laced paint by hand. They would place the brushes in their mouths to wet them to get the finest point possible. Some also painted their fingernails and teeth with the substance. The radioactivity ate away at their teeth and jaws. The founder of the company died protesting that there were no harmful effects from the paint. No joke.

Uranium glass, used for colorful marbles, and those water pitchers, contains a very *small* amount of radioactive material. Knowing what we know now, this seems ridiculous. But, hey, those were the times when cigarette companies were using doctors and Hollywood actors to promote the benefits of smoking in their ads.

Uranium was also used for Fiestaware, the popular brand of ceramic dishes and bowls. Before the early 1940's, the orange-colored line was made with uranium in the glaze. This added new meaning to serving a meal on a *hot* plate.

Unbelievably, this same toxic ore was used in children's "Atomic Energy" chemistry sets sold by Chemcraft in the 1950's. Radioactivity was really popular back then, and apparently, it seemed like a good idea to introduce it to kids early. These "play" chemistry sets may still be found on eBay. I personally would consult a reference book about radioactive collectibles before I placed a bid.

Kevin and I proceeded, with great caution, further down the old mining road. Kevin was dictating another chapter into his small digital recorder for his latest book, so I gave him a sizeable lead for privacy. With the twists and turns of the canyon, I would occasionally lose sight of him ahead of me. By the time I reached a place where the trail branched off to follow a shale ridge down to a sandy-bottom wash, I lost him altogether.

I'll let Kevin tell what happened next:

> "In the desert, wilderness trails aren't always well marked. Sometimes, you'll find a few sticks laid down as an arrow pointing to a turn in a side-wash; other times, a small stack of rocks tells hikers to 'turn here.' But if you don't spot these little signs, you might go down the wrong path and end up in trouble.
>
> On this long hike in Lathrop Canyon, Tim and I walked at a distance from each other, so I could dictate new book chapters. We were the first hikers to come down this trail in days, perhaps weeks; we saw no footprints in the snow or in the muddy snowmelt on the cliff side. Once down the rock fall, the trail became moderate, and I wandered well ahead of Tim, dictating a particularly intense part of my next novel. The scene was going quite well, though my characters weren't having a very happy time of it, and I walked and walked, following a low ridge, traveling in what seemed to be the obvious direction.
>
> Until, in the still desert air, I heard a whistle and a distant shout.
>
> I looked around and spotted Tim waving from a ridge on the other side of the canyon. He cupped his hands around his mouth and shouted very clearly, 'The trail's over here!'
>
> I looked around and realized that I was just following the lay of the land, taking the easiest route. Focused on my story, I must have missed an important turn somewhere. I backtracked the way I had come, too rattled to keep writing for the moment (thereby giving my characters a brief reprieve from their fates). After

about a quarter mile, I spotted where I had gone wrong—a cairn of rocks indicating a turn. Too preoccupied with other things, I had missed the direction sign.

I do my best writing when I'm in 'the zone,' but I still need to pay attention to the world around me, notice important road signs, and whether I'm off course. I could have wandered off into the desert for miles without realizing the error. Fortunately, Tim had spotted me going astray, and I was able to do a route correction."

Without a little help from a friend—or brother-in-law—Kevin's story from Lathrop Trail might have been quite a different one! (Yet, some of his book characters may have then survived.) Rejoined, we continued on the correct route down the wash to the White Rim Road. The White Rim Road—so named for its rock sediment color at the edge before another deep canyon drop off—is a rugged, 4-wheel drive, 100-mile Jeep and mountain bike road on a shelf around the base of the Island in the Sky.

On a previous trip to Canyonlands, we had already hiked the seven-mile round trip from the White Rim Road down to the Colorado River. This section of the Lathrop Trail extends all the way down to the river, and was turned into a sandy Jeep trail around 1953. The uranium prospectors used the road to obtain water from the Colorado for their mining operations. We took a short break for a trail-snack lunch while enjoying the impressive view of the Airport Tower monolith dominating the landscape.

Honored History

Our return climb back up the rockslide and cliffy area was as difficult as we anticipated. Going was slow and arduous, but we still topped the rim by mid-afternoon. Earlier that morning, on our way to the mesa rim, we had seen an old tin shed about 150 yards off the trail. This seemed worth exploring as a quick side trip before we finished the snow-covered meadow back to our truck. We didn't have reason to believe this small building was radioactive.

From our trail description literature, we learned that this shed was used by Basque sheep ranchers to store supplies before packing their flock down the trail for their seasonal grazing. What a challenge the trail down must have been for sheepherders' packhorses decades ago! Most of the trails that we use today from Island in the Sky to the White Rim Road plateau were made by ranchers to get to winter pasture. They were still used by the sheep ranchers until the 1960's when Canyonlands became a national park.

Old Basque shepherd's building, Island in the Sky mesa, Canyonlands, Utah.

Some say the Basques first arrived in the New World as part of Christopher Columbus' crew. The emigration to North and South America in the late 1800's was brought about by poor economic conditions in the Basque homeland in the Pyrenees Mountains in Northeastern Spain and Southeastern France, and also by the political turmoil of the Spanish Civil War. Most of the Basque settlers drifted to the American West, where they could continue their traditional livelihood as sheepherders.

Basque immigrants earned the reputation as the most diligent, hardworking, conscientious and capable ranch workers available. When driving the highways and byways of the high desert ranges of the West, one has to ponder how anyone could possibly live there, let alone live the demanding life as a shepherd. The Basques took the jobs because of the economic opportunity, and tended flocks for months on end in this harsh, desolate environment. This had to be far worse than my department store job in college.

The Basque shepherds were tough, hardy individuals, but their isolation in the vast, empty country made adjusting to their new life in America difficult. This must have been one of the loneliest professions in the world (just ahead of unpublished author).

But the Basques were real stockmen and could be counted on to stay long periods alone and not leave their flocks. They demonstrated what a skill it was to handle range sheep with only a sheepdog for a companion and no fences or night corrals. The herders had to be on constant guard against predators like mountain lions, coyotes, and bears. And, the sheepherders had to keep the sheep moving to fresh water and good grazing areas.

Kevin and I were impressed with the challenges these Basque shepherds faced, their work ethic, and their business integrity throughout a 150-year story. They were viewed and respected throughout this region as one of its unique cultural and economic assets.

By the 1960's, the U. S. sheep industry waned for a variety of reasons. Consequently, most Basques moved off the ranges to other careers, returned to their homeland with improved economic conditions, or shifted their shepherding efforts to Latin America. Their honored history and reputation lives on.

What a contrast in stories and legacies between the Basque shepherds and the uranium industries in the Canyonlands region.

Patrick Ricketts says, "Everyone has a story, make your own worth telling." One would hope the story told is a good one.

This small tale ended well. We made it back to our car before dark, and the return trek across the snow meadow was made easier by stepping into our previous tracks.

But, I was left with some personal questions: What's my story going to be? How will it end? Who will tell the story, and for what reasons? I don't know entirely. But, with the time I have left, there are still life trail opportunities to be explored, and new chapters to be written.

Conclusion

I should have warned you before you read this book: get me started sharing my 14er experiences and I'll talk your ear off, whether you want me to or not. Ask me about the Moab region—what to see and do, what trails to explore, what time of day is best for photography—and two hours later, I'll just be revving up. I love to talk about my outdoor adventures, and to listen to the tales of others.

My intent with this book was not only to share my experiences, but to entertain, inform, educate (learning from my goofball mistakes), and to motivate. My hope is that readers will be inspired to get up off the couch, turn off the TV, pull the kids away from their video games and smartphones and get out to make their own stories.

Admittedly, not all of my trail hiking or climbing is for everyone (just ask the folks who will never go out with me again). I've made some aggressive and extreme choices for my *wild*erness expeditions. That's fine for some; not so much for others. You don't have to do crazy things like me to have a great time outdoors. Not everyone can travel to Colorado and Utah. Understandably, young families have small children, and some folks are beyond their hiking years.

I encourage those interested in spending time in nature to do what they *can* to get outside. City parks and local nature trails can be a wonderful place to spend time with family on a warm afternoon. Most cities have some kind of biking trail system. Many have designated open spaces to enjoy. Go to the lake. Go to the beach. Go to the hills or forests or canyons. Go to the arboretum. Go anywhere. But go.

Many national, state, and regional parks have handicapped access. Some nature parks have value-added interpretive trails—

informative for young and old—with some even set up for the blind. There really are ways for everybody to enjoy the great outdoors, regardless of age, medical problems, phobias, disabilities, disposition, time or energy, family and work obligations, or stage/change of life issues. Make the effort and you may be surprised at the outcome.

You might be able to do more than you think you can. I did. When I first started climbing the Colorado 14ers, I thought it was the hardest thing I had ever done in my life. There were times I wanted to quit (out of fatigue, uncertainty, or fear). But I didn't quit. I kept trying, kept going, kept climbing. Regardless of your outdoor activity choice, if you have the desire and the will, and are eager to try, the reward will be worth the challenge.

For me, beyond enjoying the obvious beauty, the wilderness can be a refuge from the noise and clutter and insanity of my life. In its purity and natural wonder, there is peace, freedom, serenity, and solace. It is good for my soul. John Muir said, "Keep close to Nature's heart ... and break clear away, once in a while, and climb a mountain or spend a week in the woods. Wash your spirit clean."

Spending time in the wilderness is a deeply spiritual experience. I no longer go out to the wilderness because I want to; I go to the wilderness because I *have* to.

Join me in the journey! There are more adventures to be lived, more stories to be told. What will your stories be?

One More Step...

To read more of my trail stories from the West, please go to my blog at:

TalesFromTheTrails.net

Or visit LIFE: Sentences—Literary observations on the human experience at:

www.lifesentences.org

Would you like to comment on the book or share your trail stories? Contact me at:

tim@TalesFromTheTrails.net

Would you like to get a book for a friend? Order at:

www.WordFirePress.com

About the Author

Tim (he thinks T.Duren sounds more impressive) **Jones**, a former Periodicals Editorial and Art Director, has worked in marketing, advertising, and publishing for more than 25 years. He currently does freelance commercial art, marketing, and advertising consulting (if he has to, when he's not hiking). Tim and Diane have raised four creative and equally adventurous children. He and Diane enjoy an active outdoor lifestyle together that includes biking, softball, snowshoeing, and exploring the many wonderful trails in their home state of Colorado.

Other WordFire Titles

Be sure to check out the growing list of other great WordFire Press titles at:

www.wordfirepress.com

www.ingramcontent.com/pod-product-compliance
Lightning Source LLC
Chambersburg PA
CBHW020411080526
44584CB00014B/1271